60 BEAUTIFUL GEOMETRIC PATTERNS
ADULT COLORING BOOK
VOLUME ONE

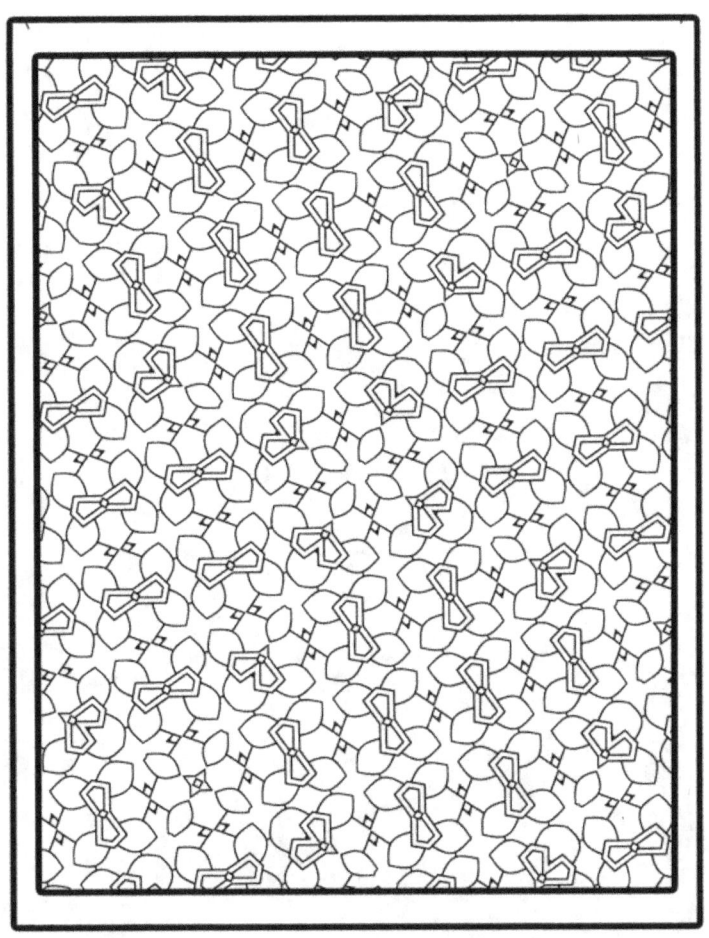

CALMOLOR
where calm and color combine

COLORING TIPS

Each image is printed on a single-sided page. Colored pencils will work perfectly, but if you would like to use markers or press heavily when coloring, place a piece of paper or thin card behind the image you would like to color to prevent bleed through. There is a blank page at the end of the book for this specific use. If you would like to take any pages out, tear carefully, or use a page perforator, which you can purchase on Amazon.

Have fun, relax and enjoy!

COLOR TEST PAGE

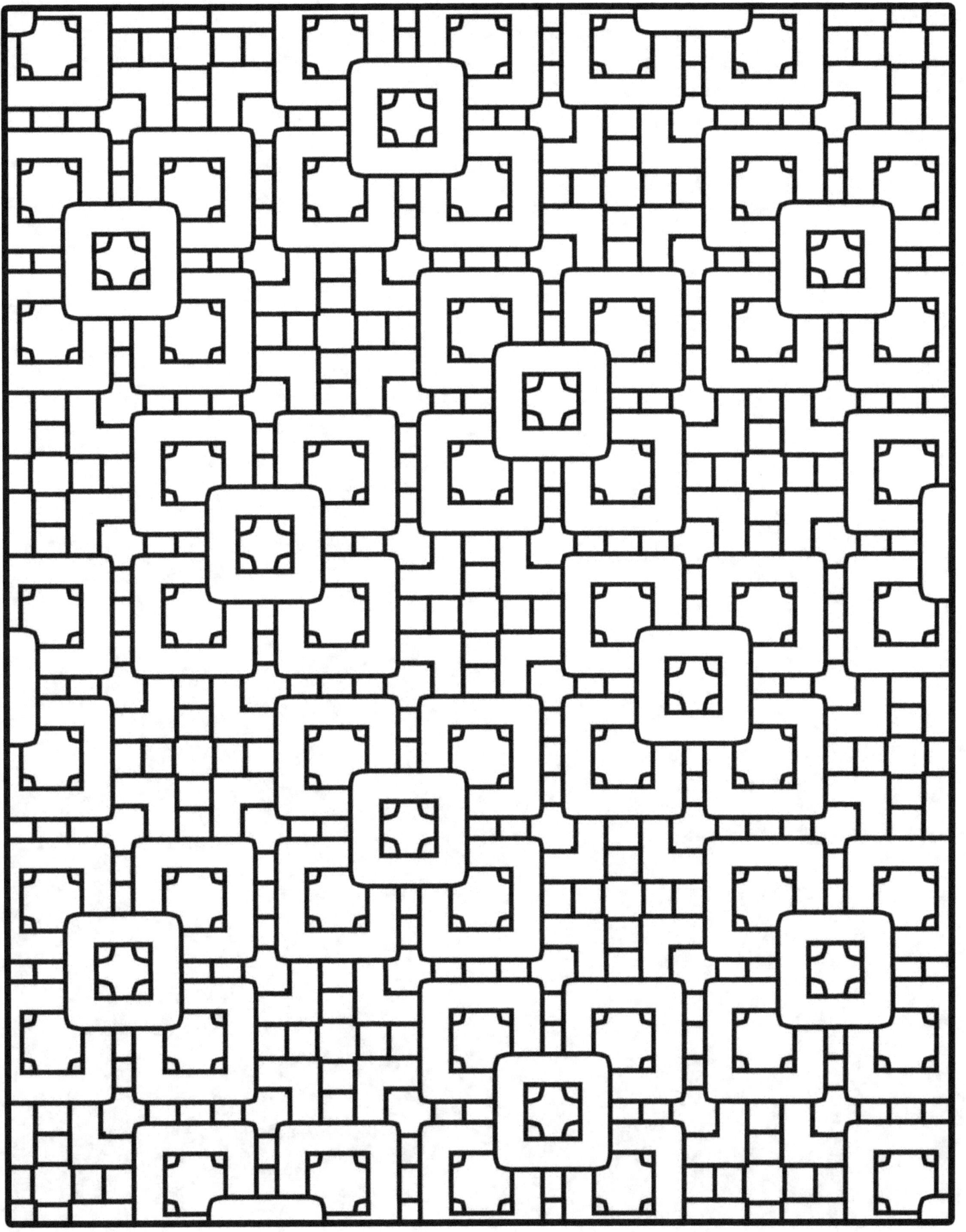

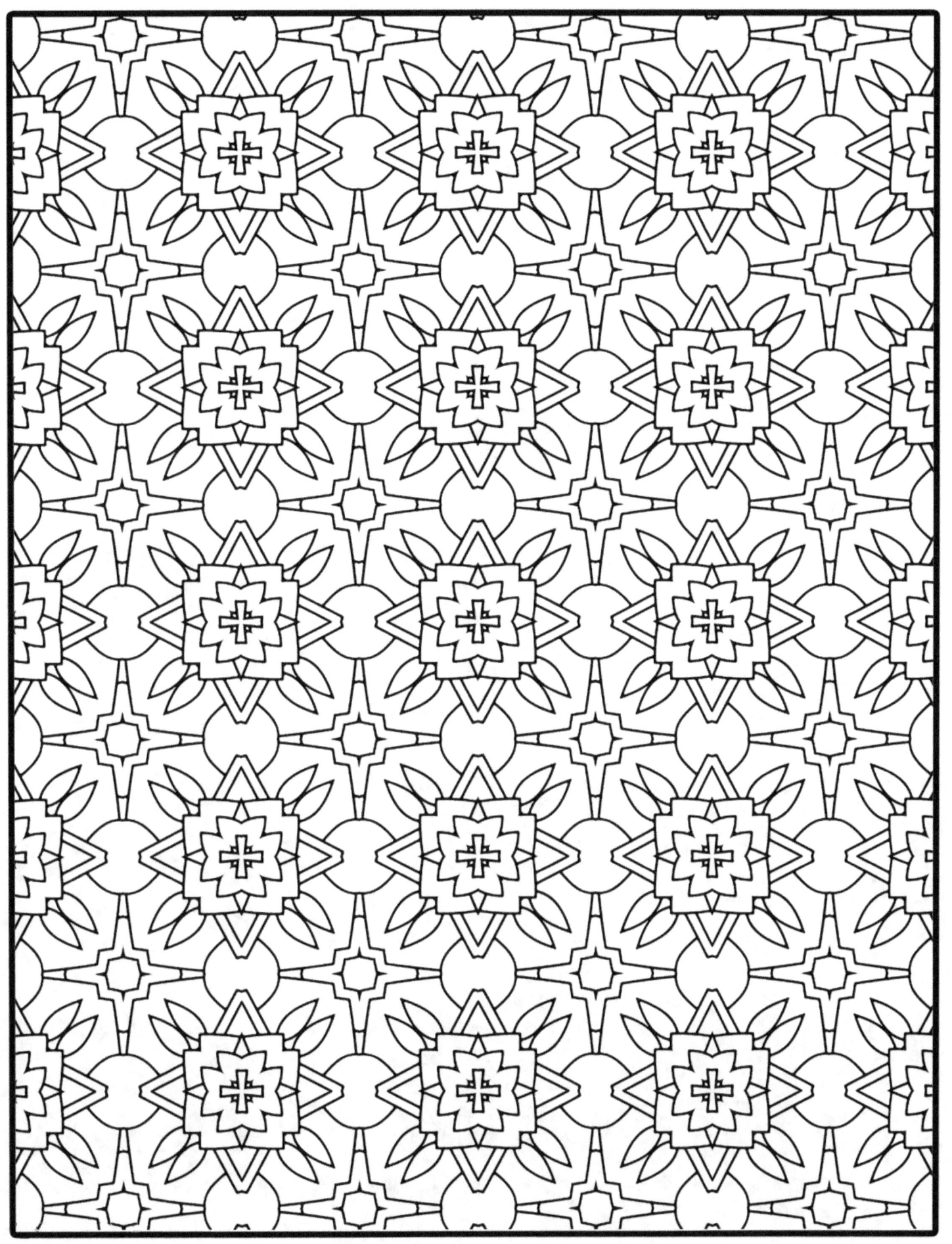

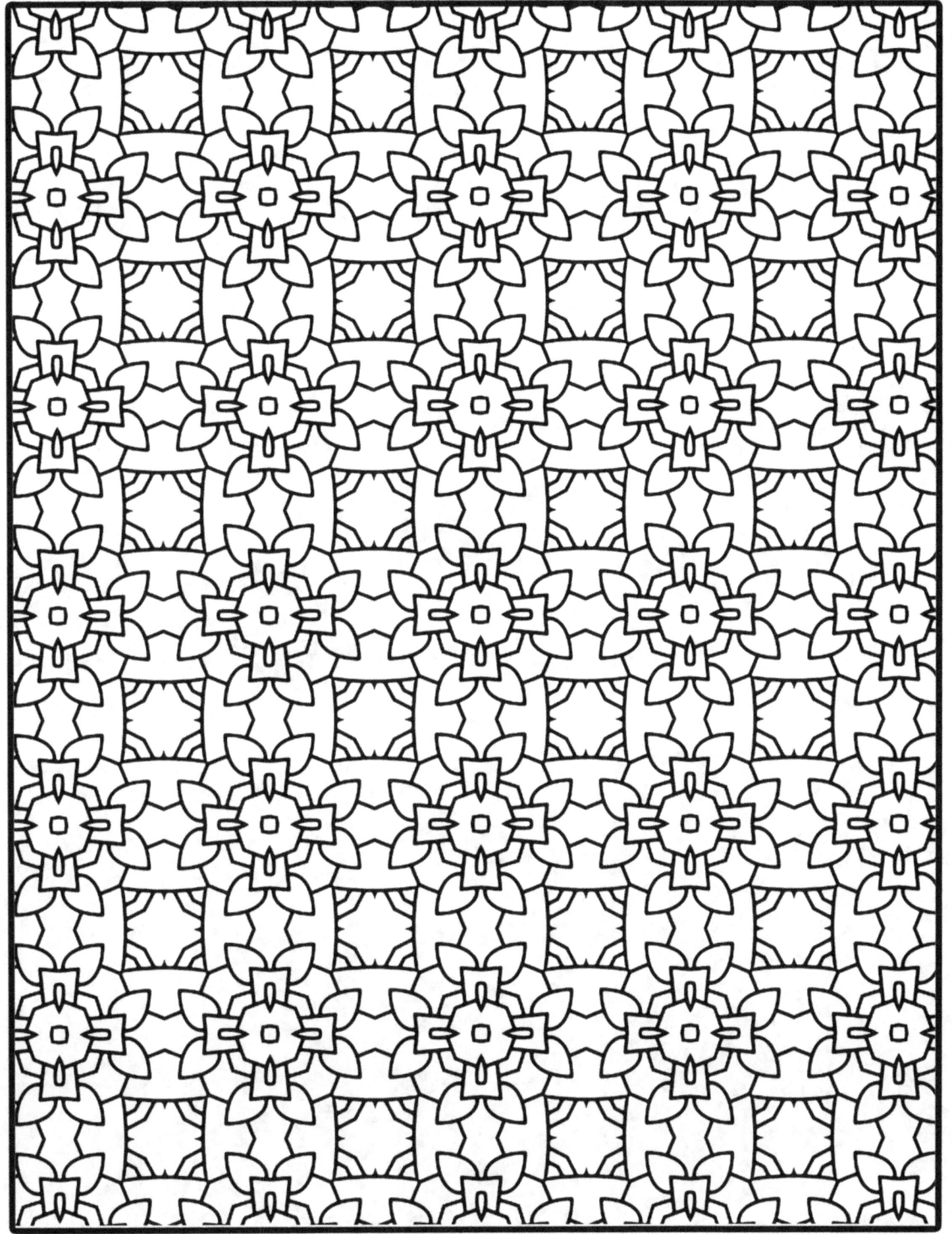

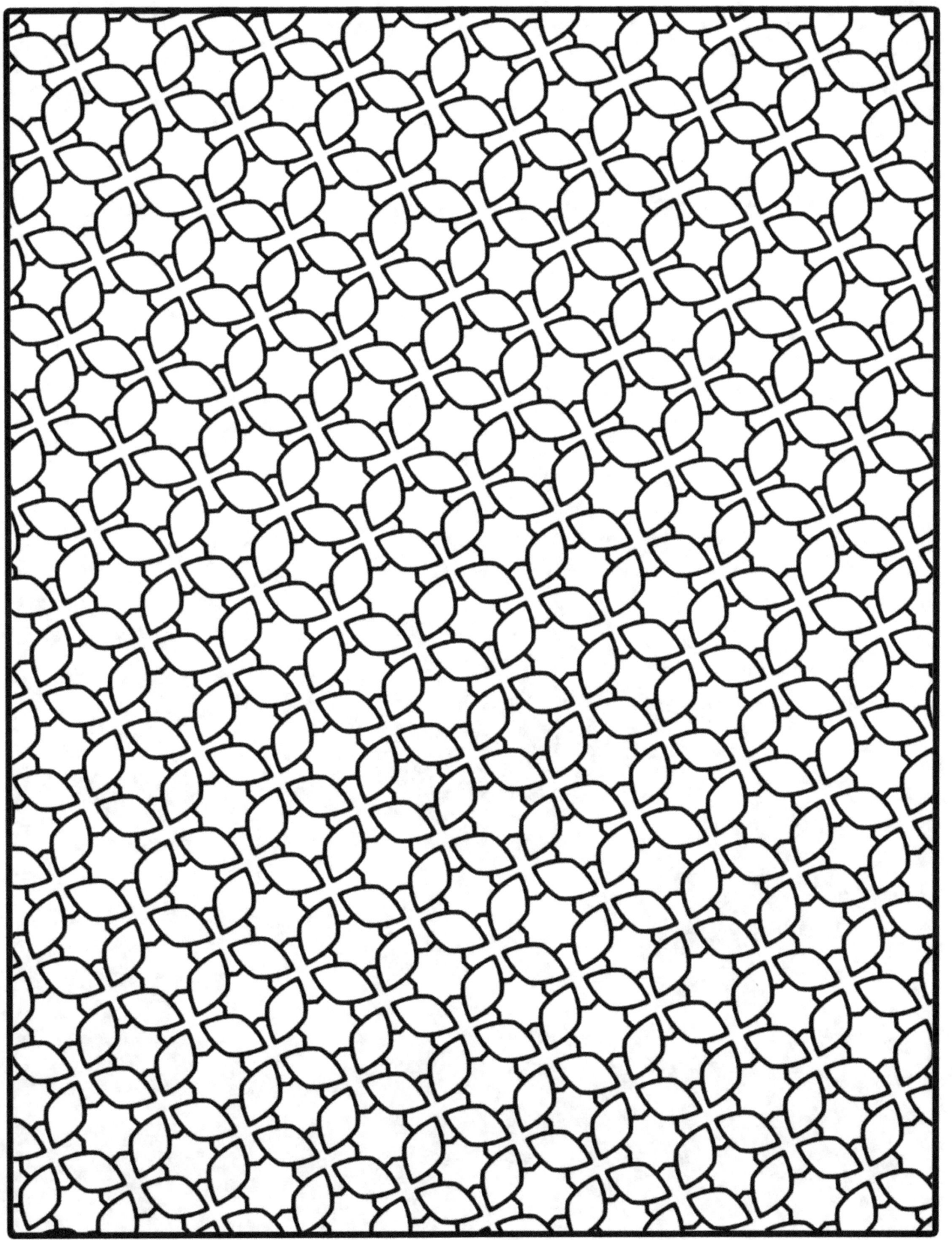

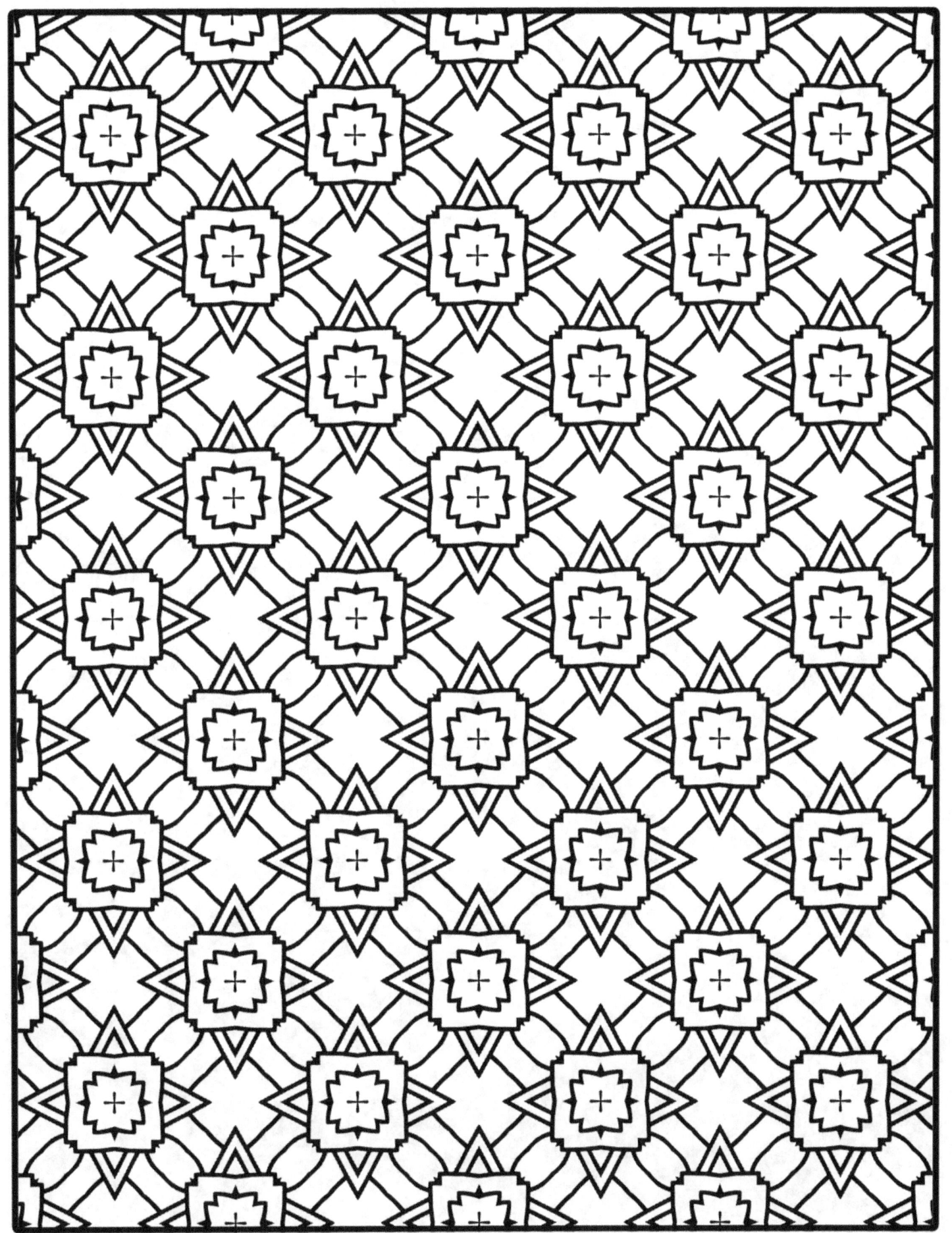

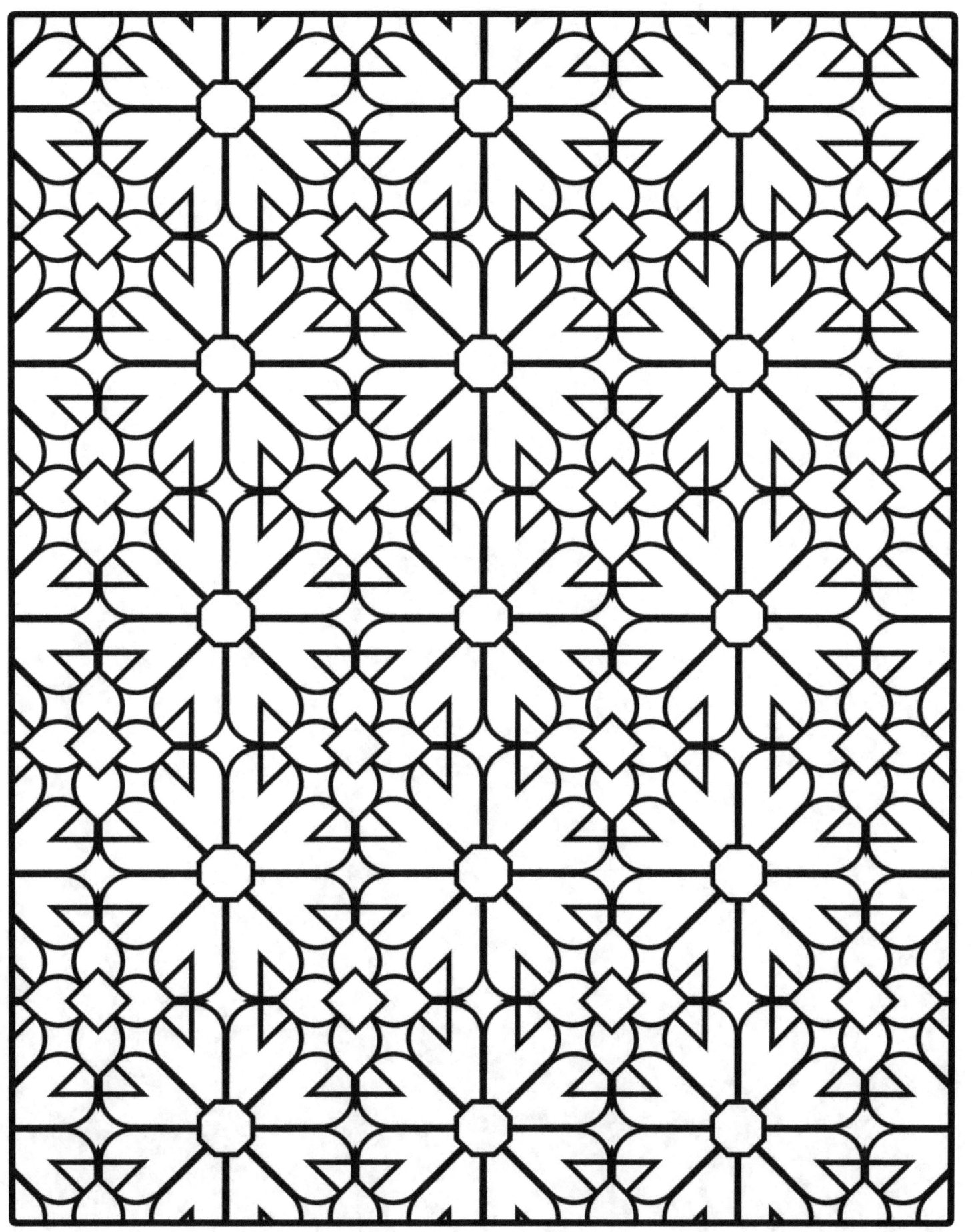

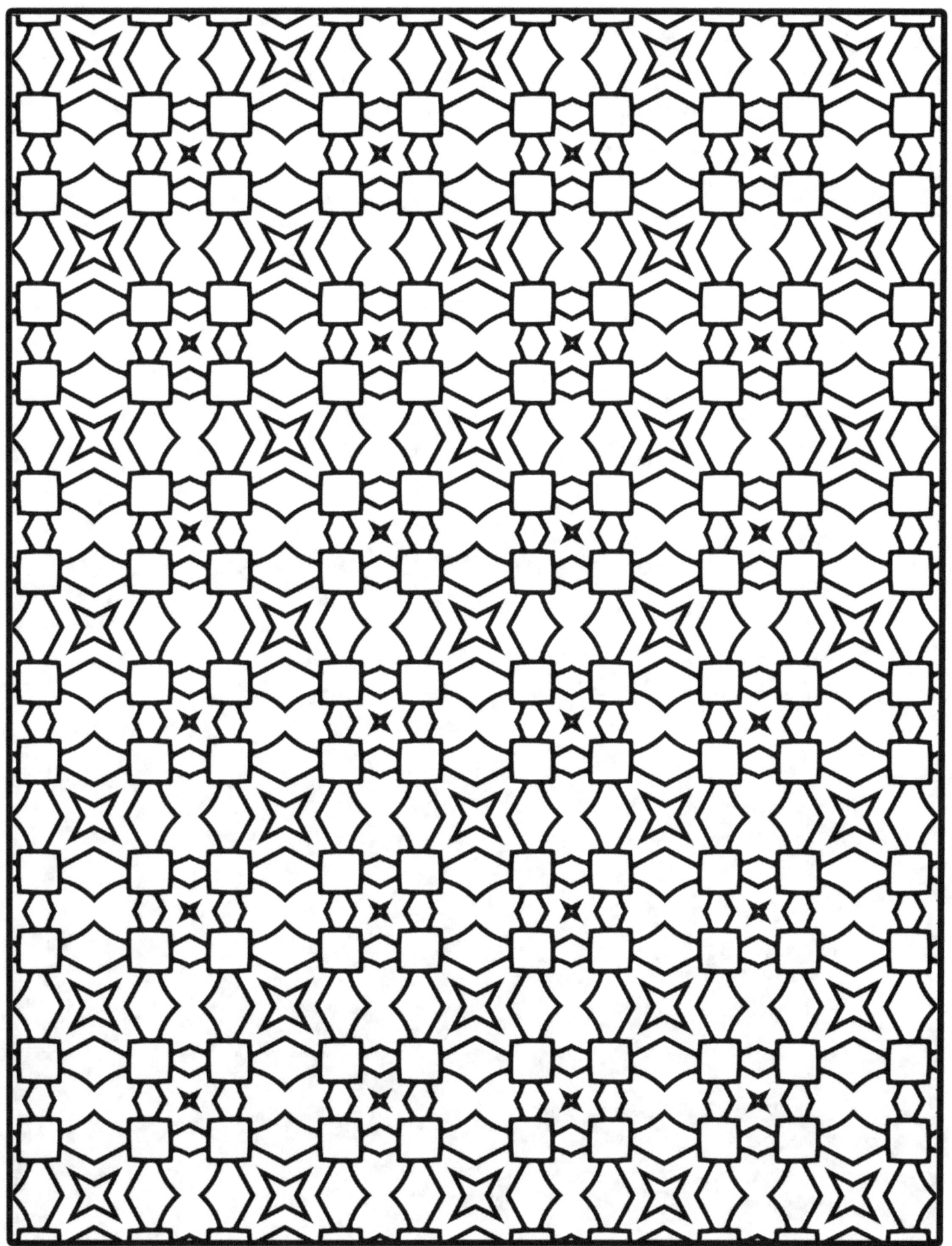

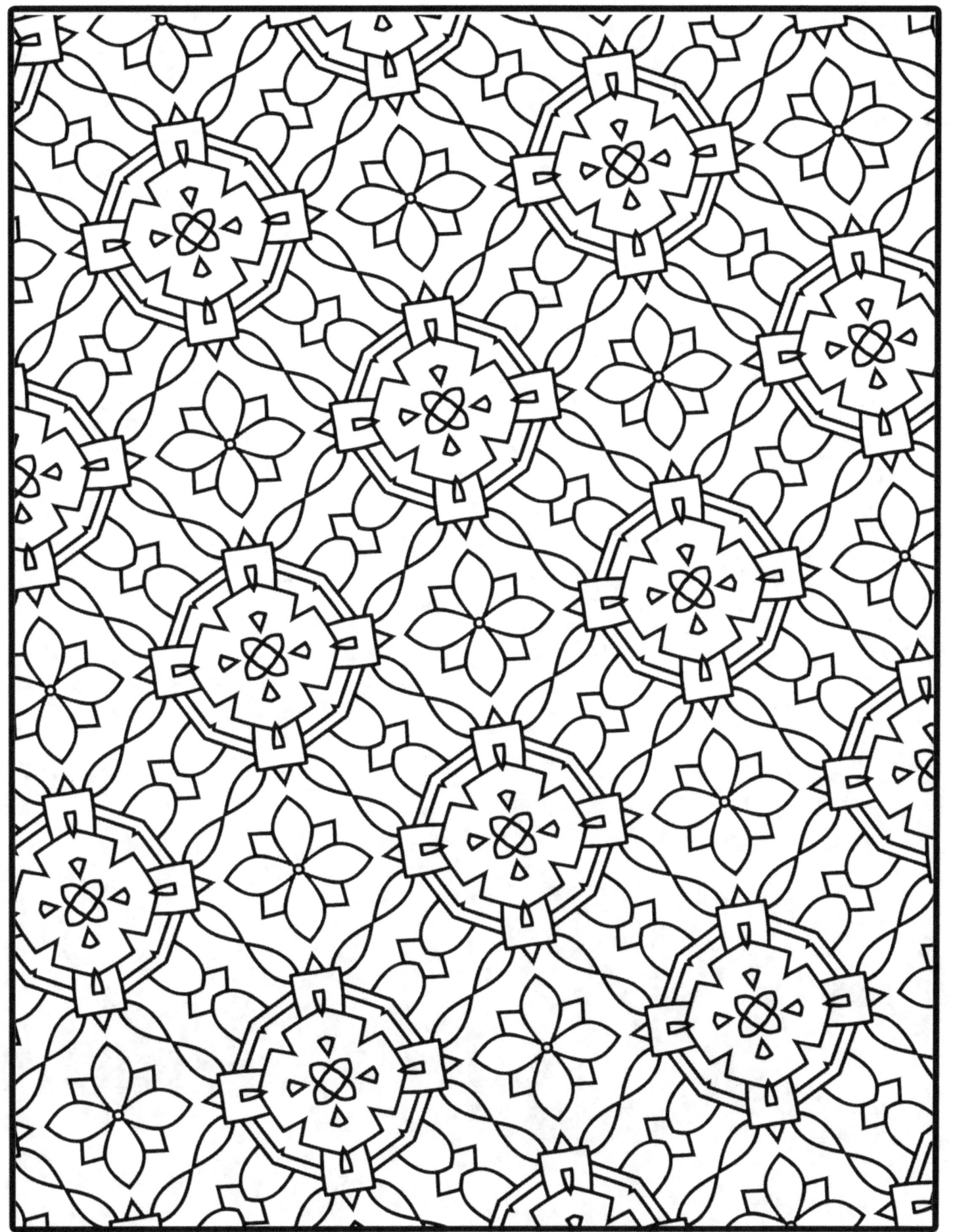

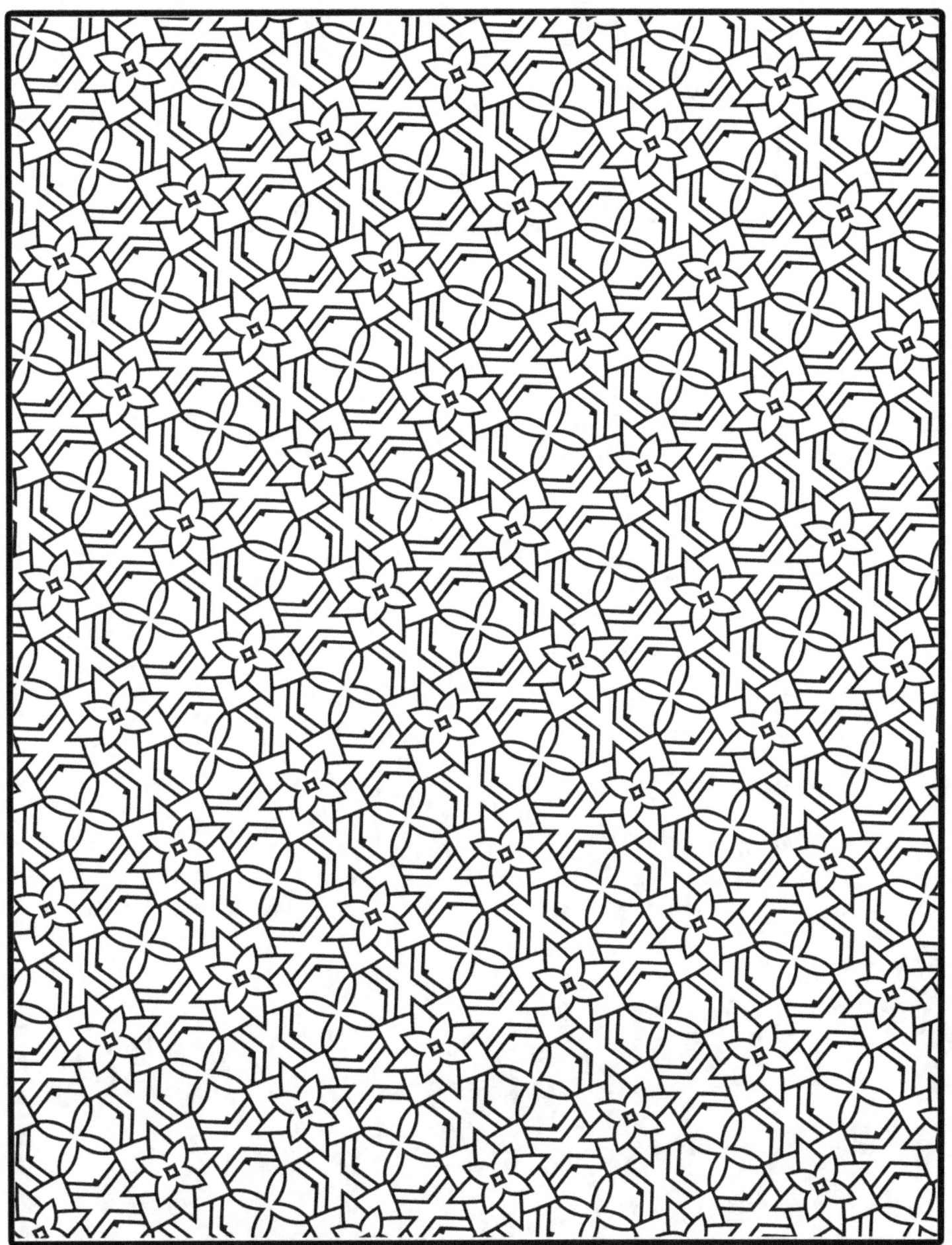

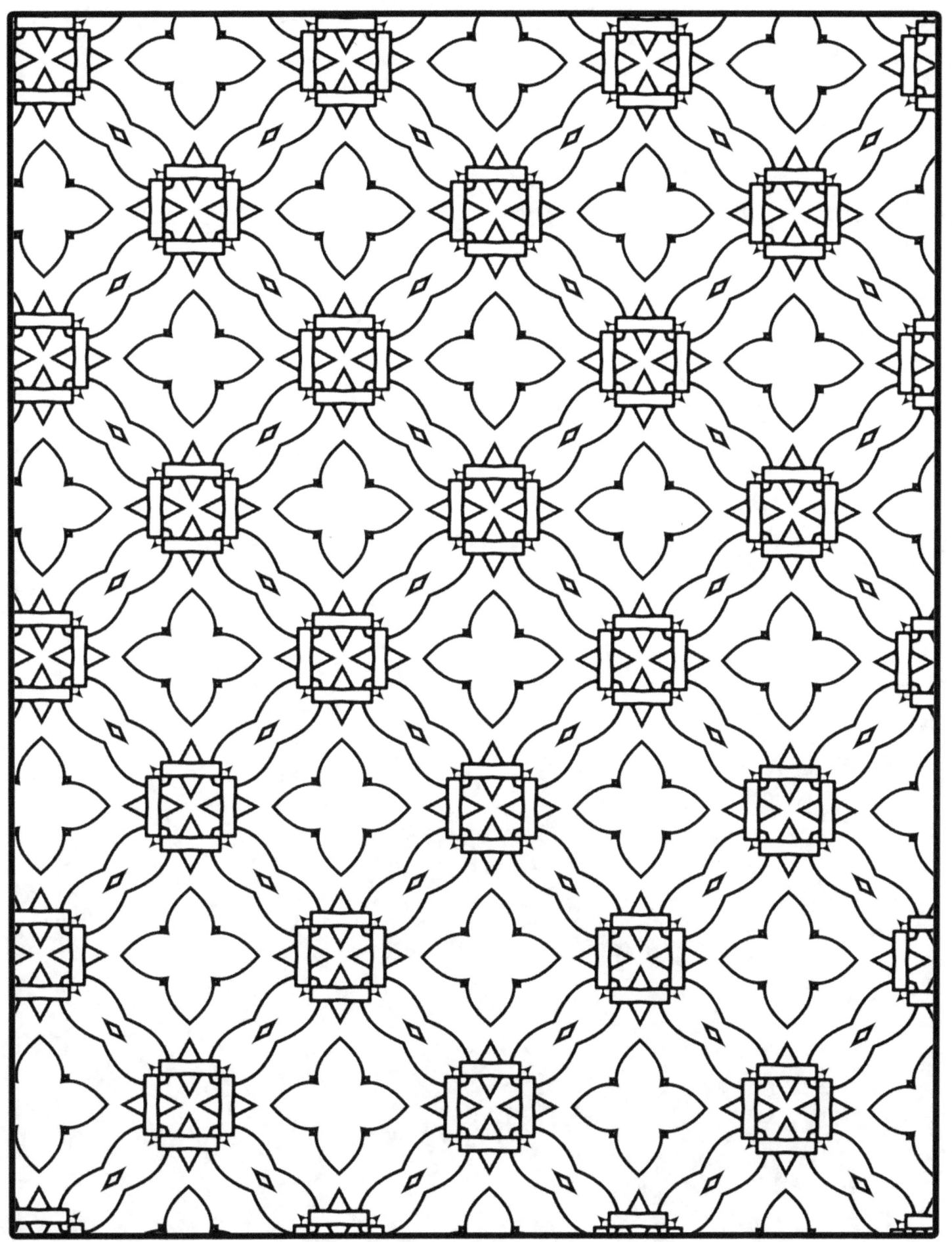

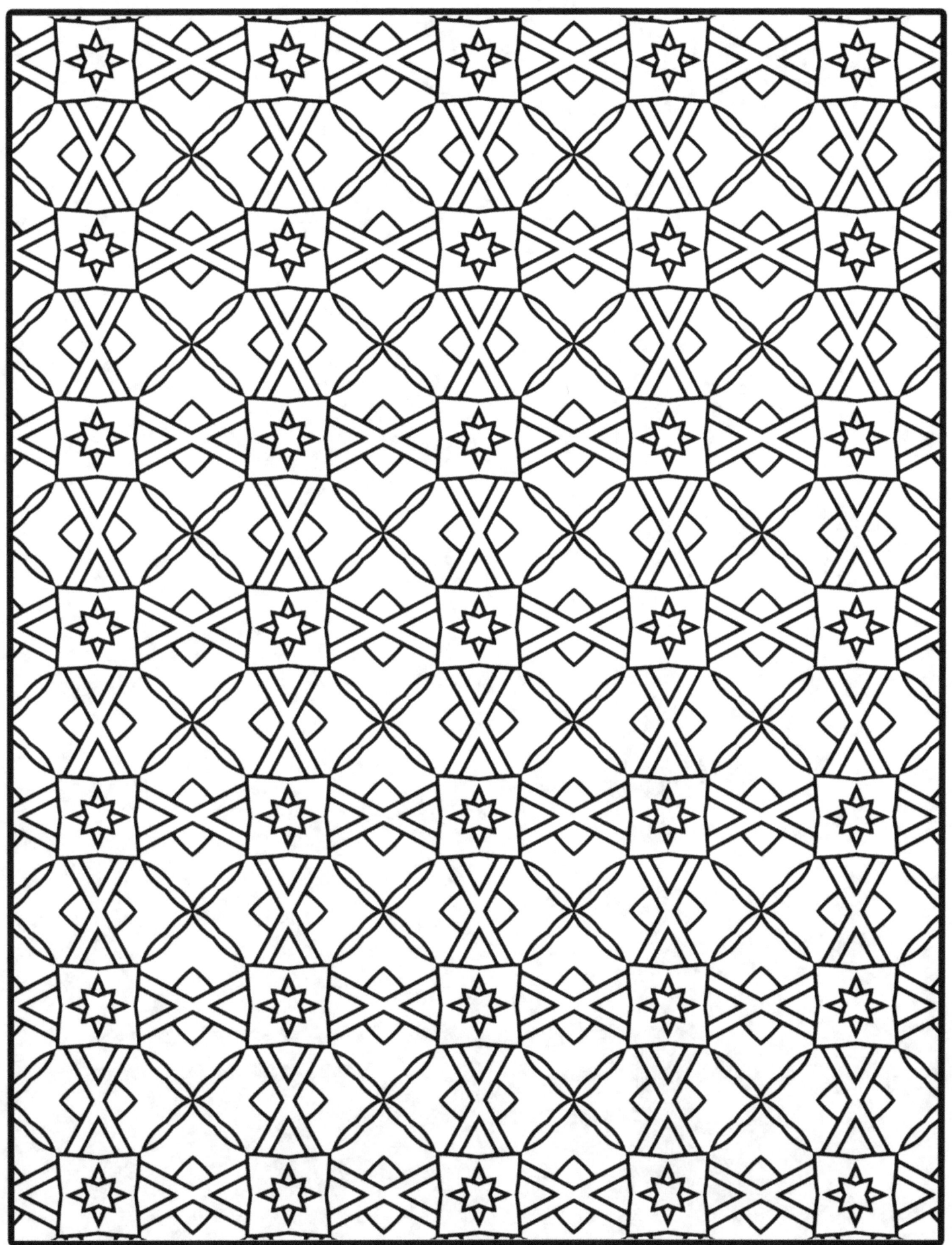

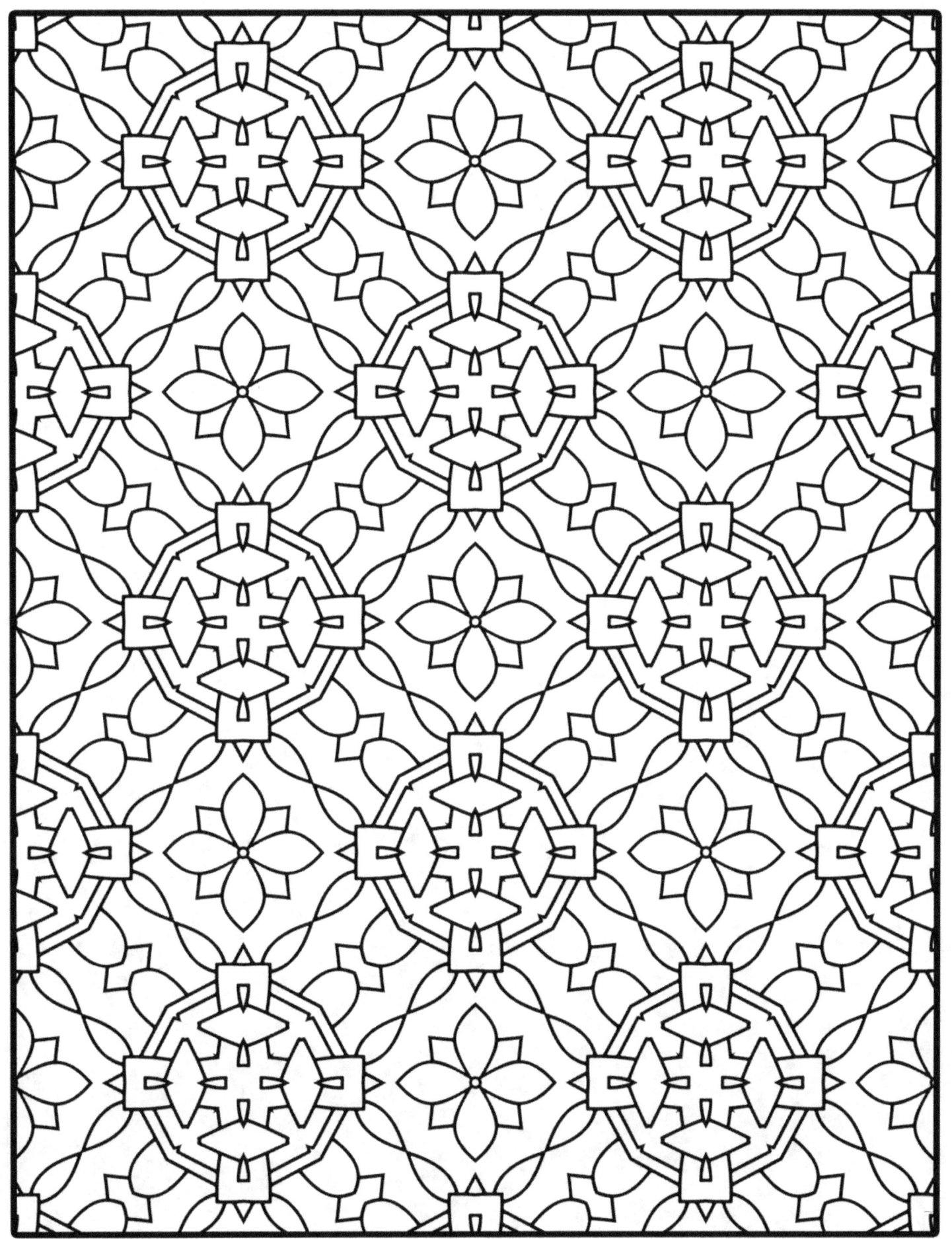

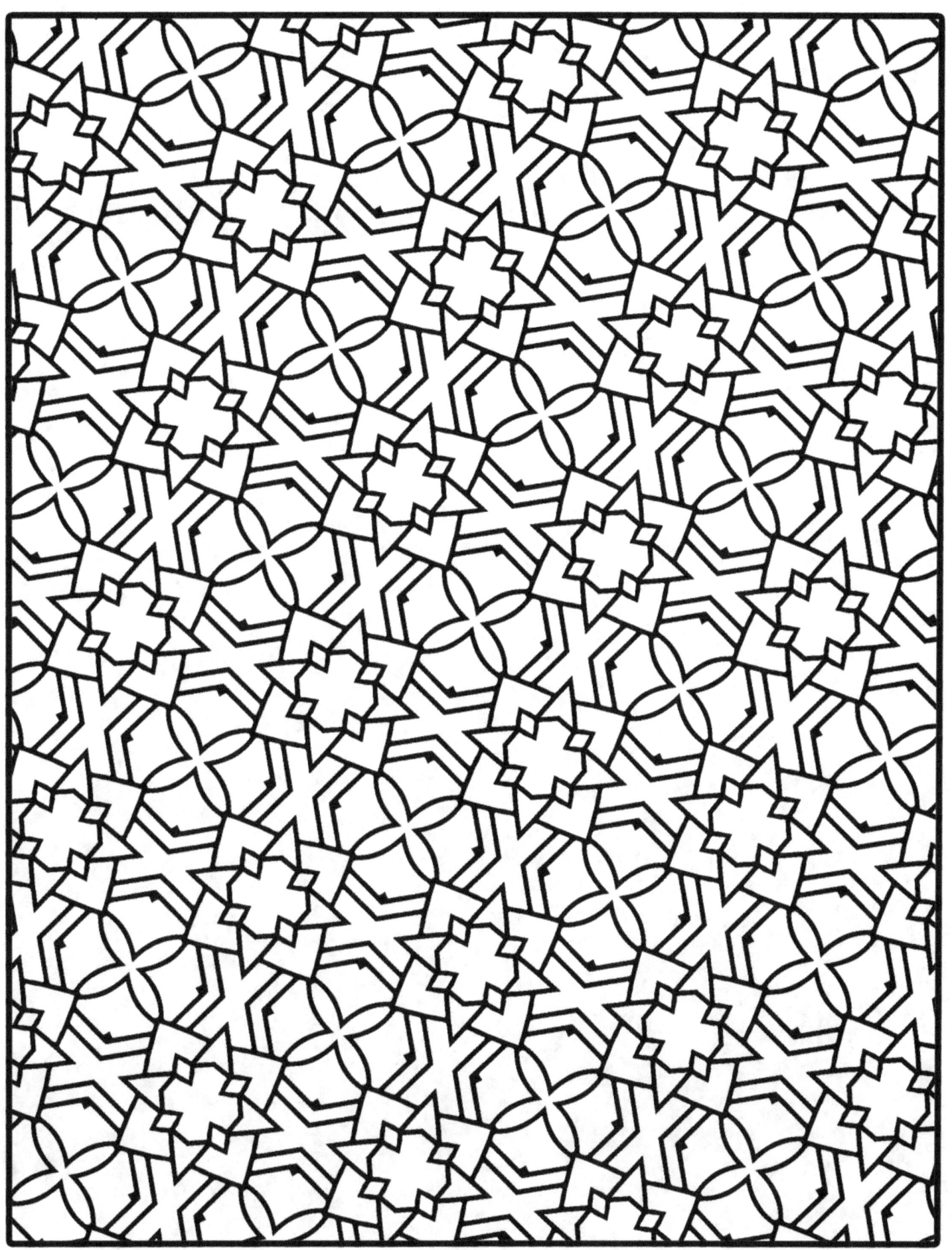

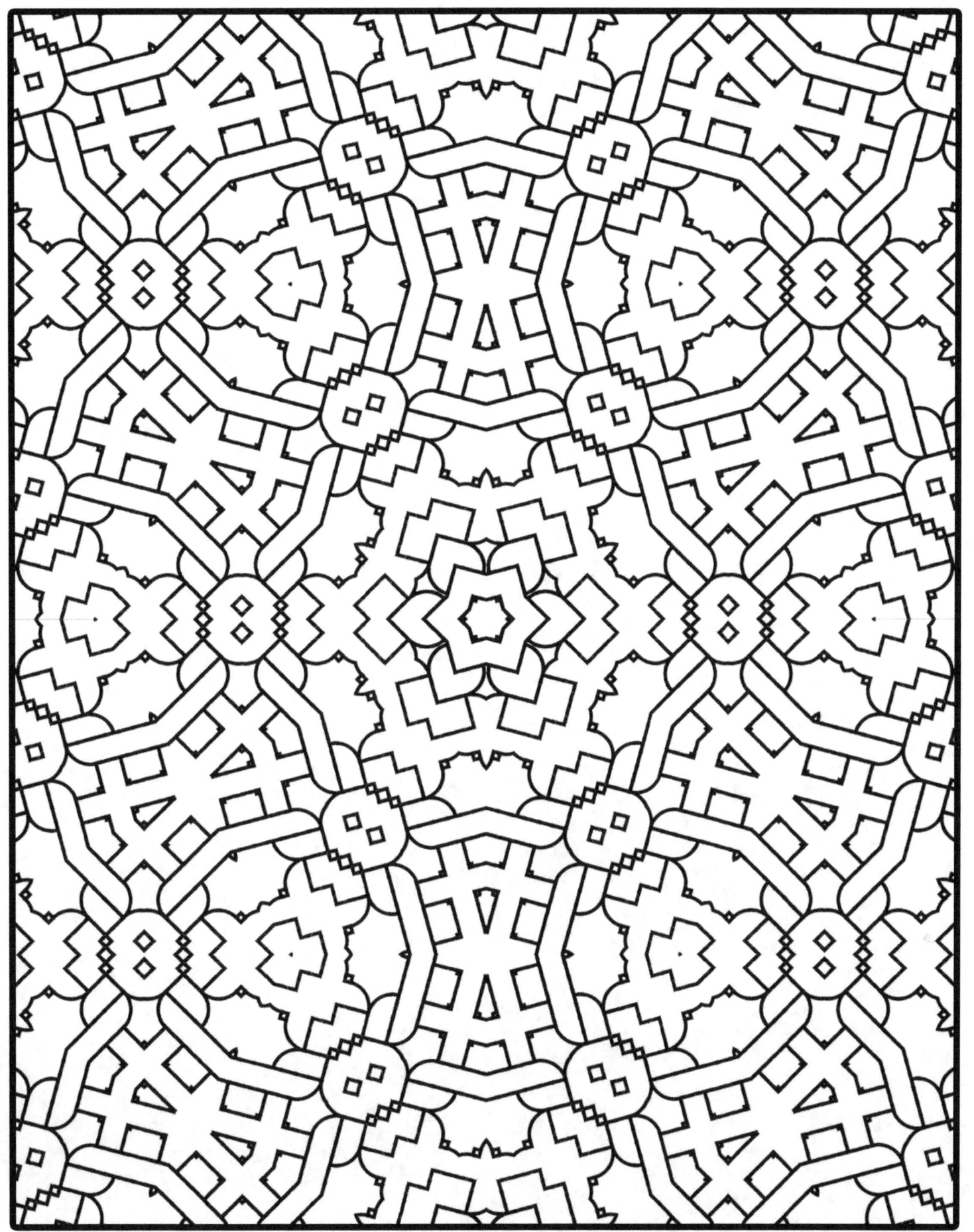

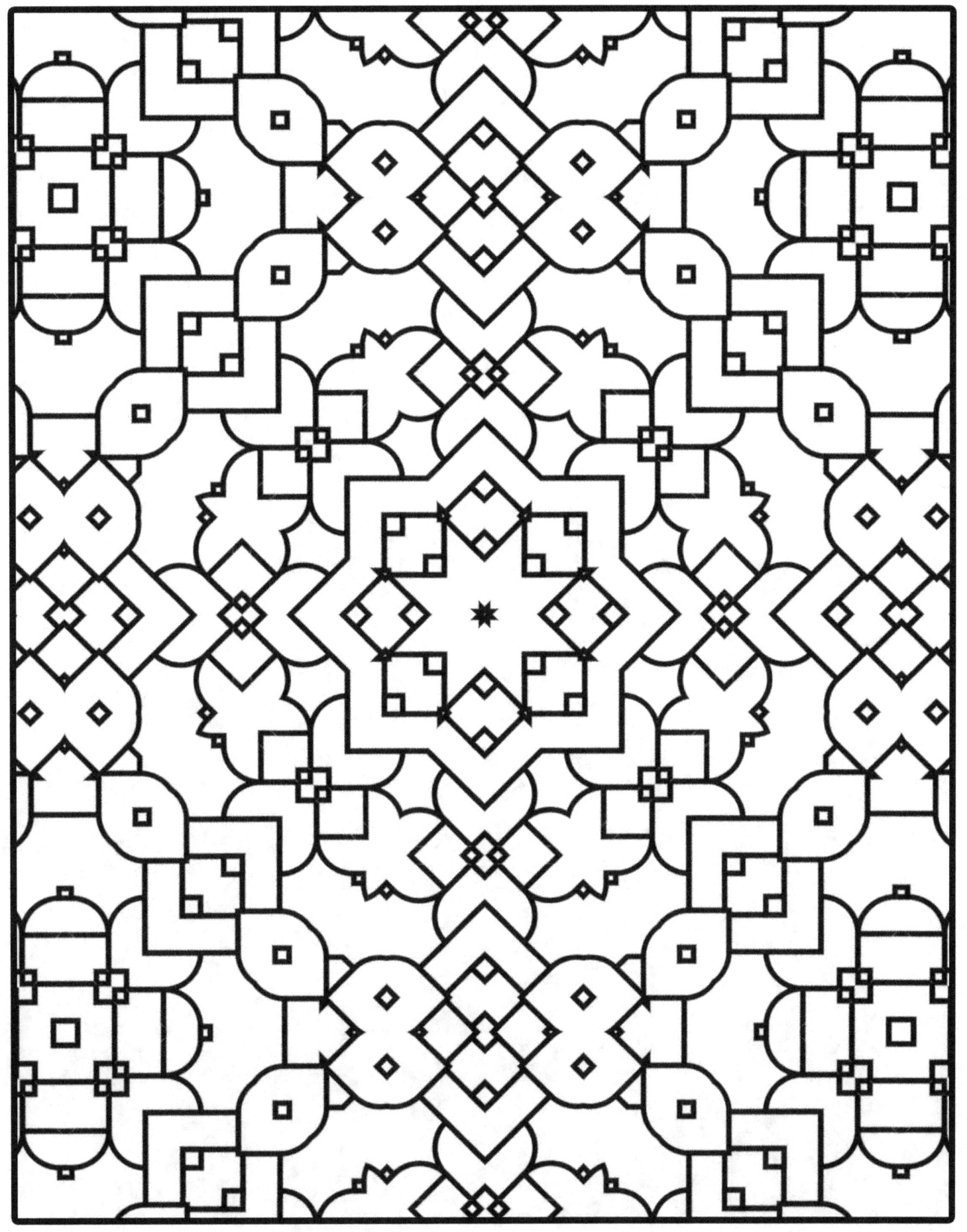

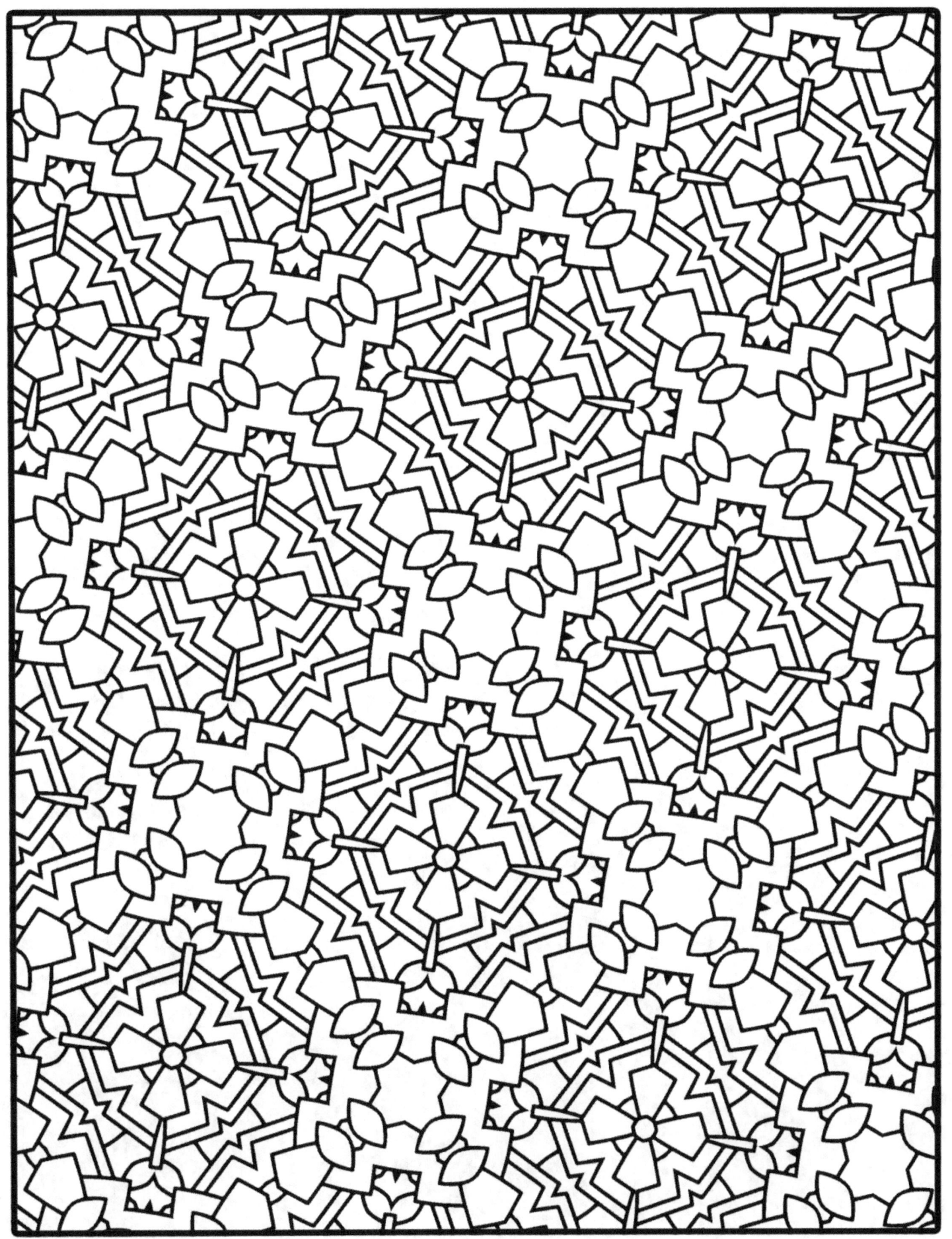

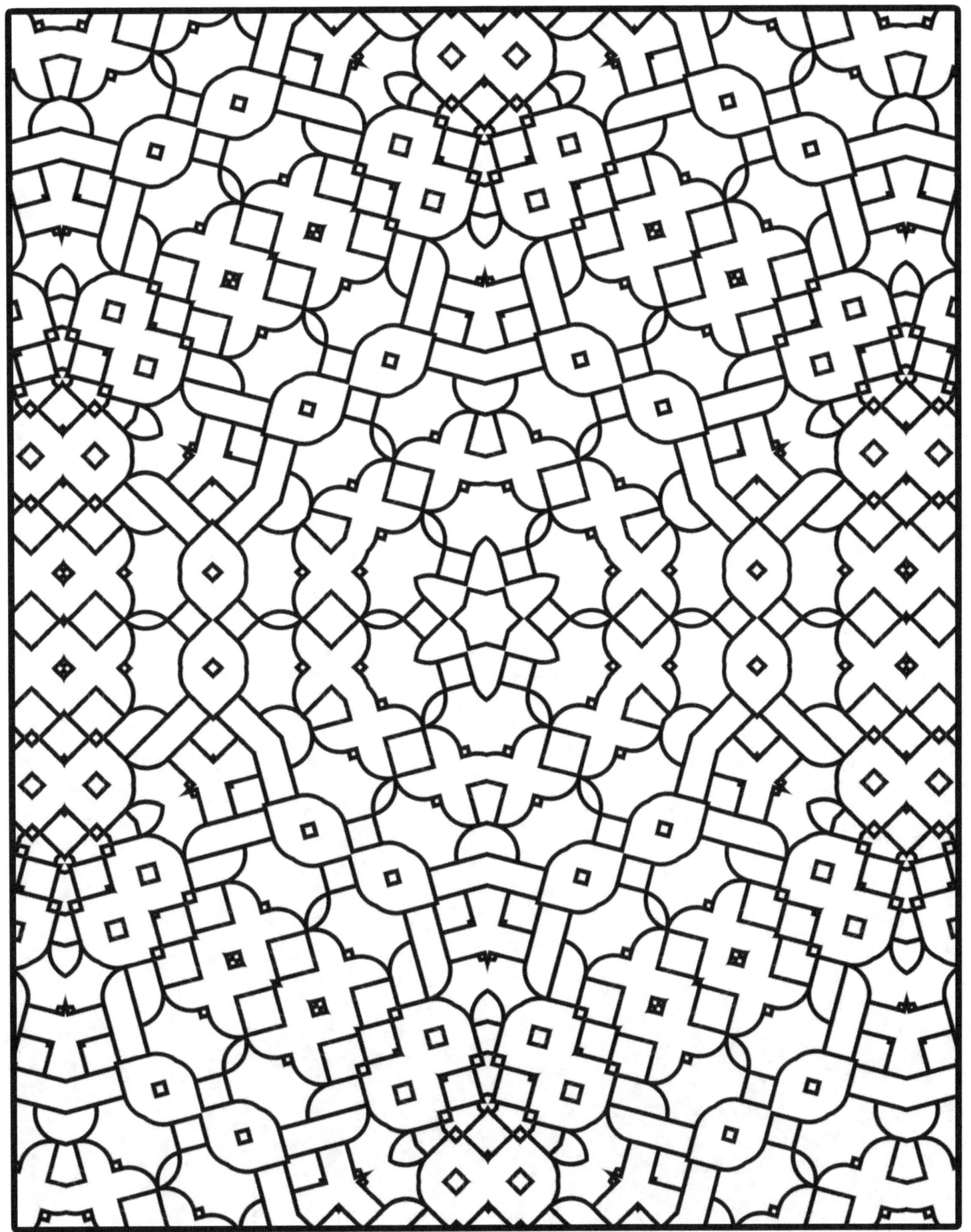

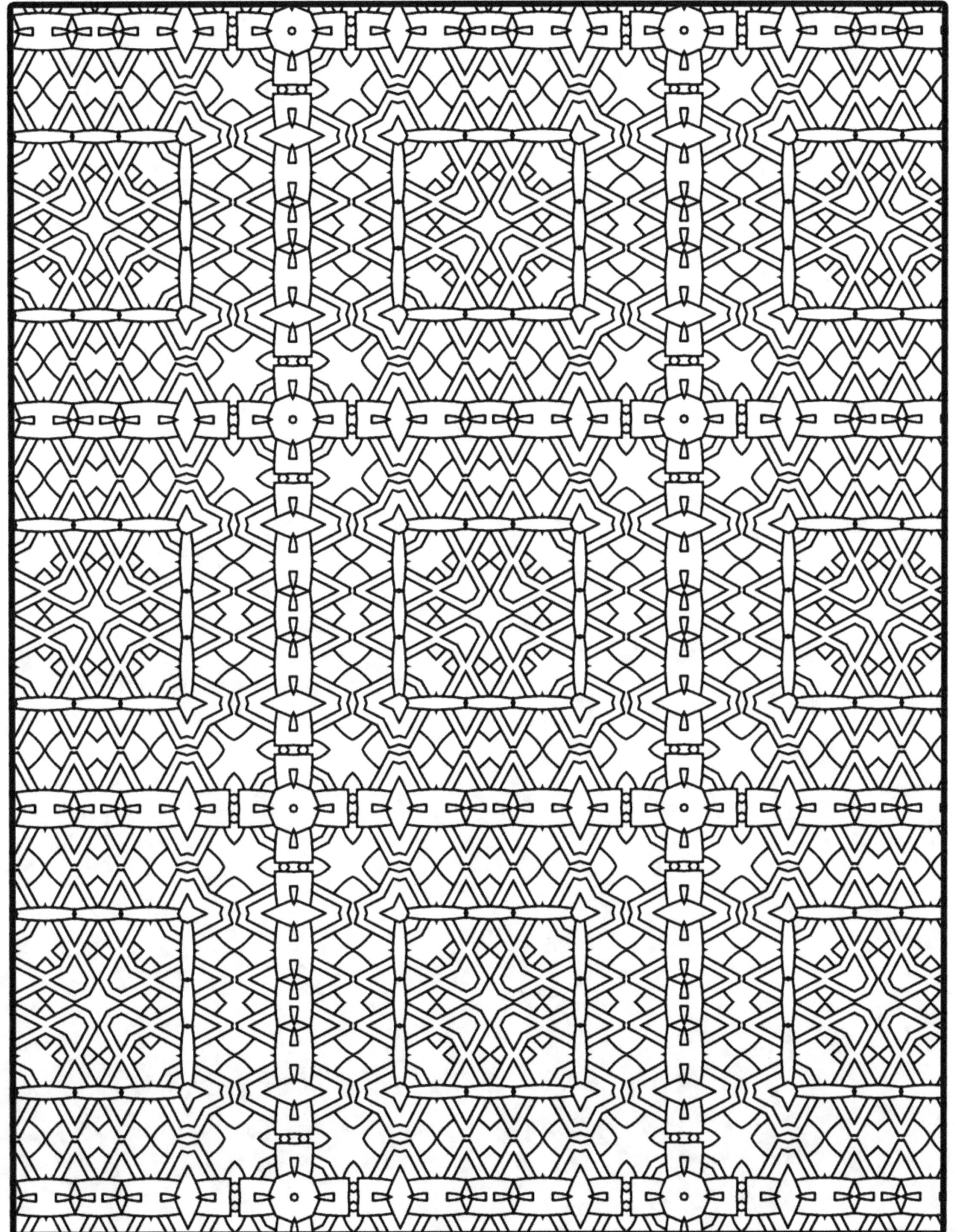

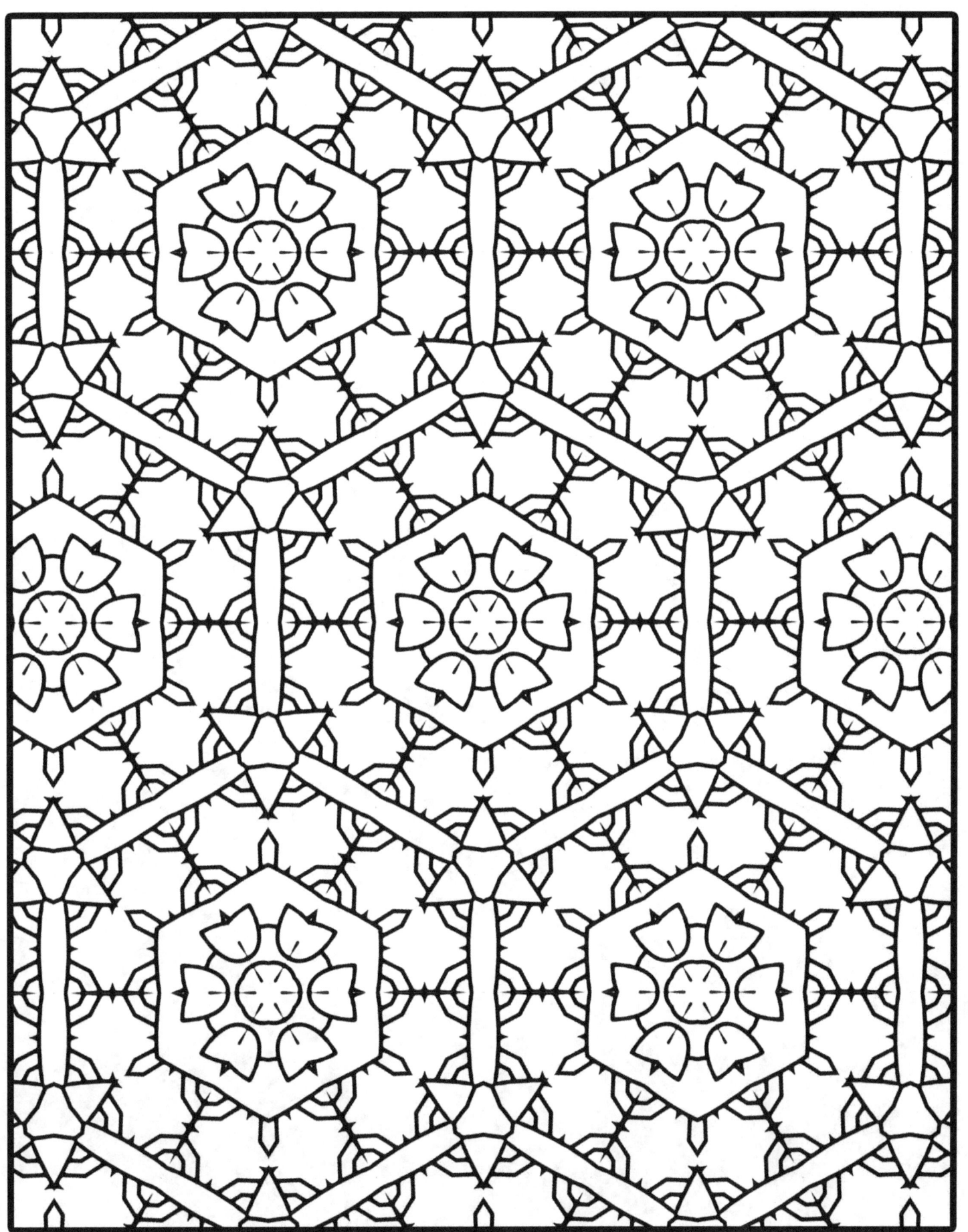

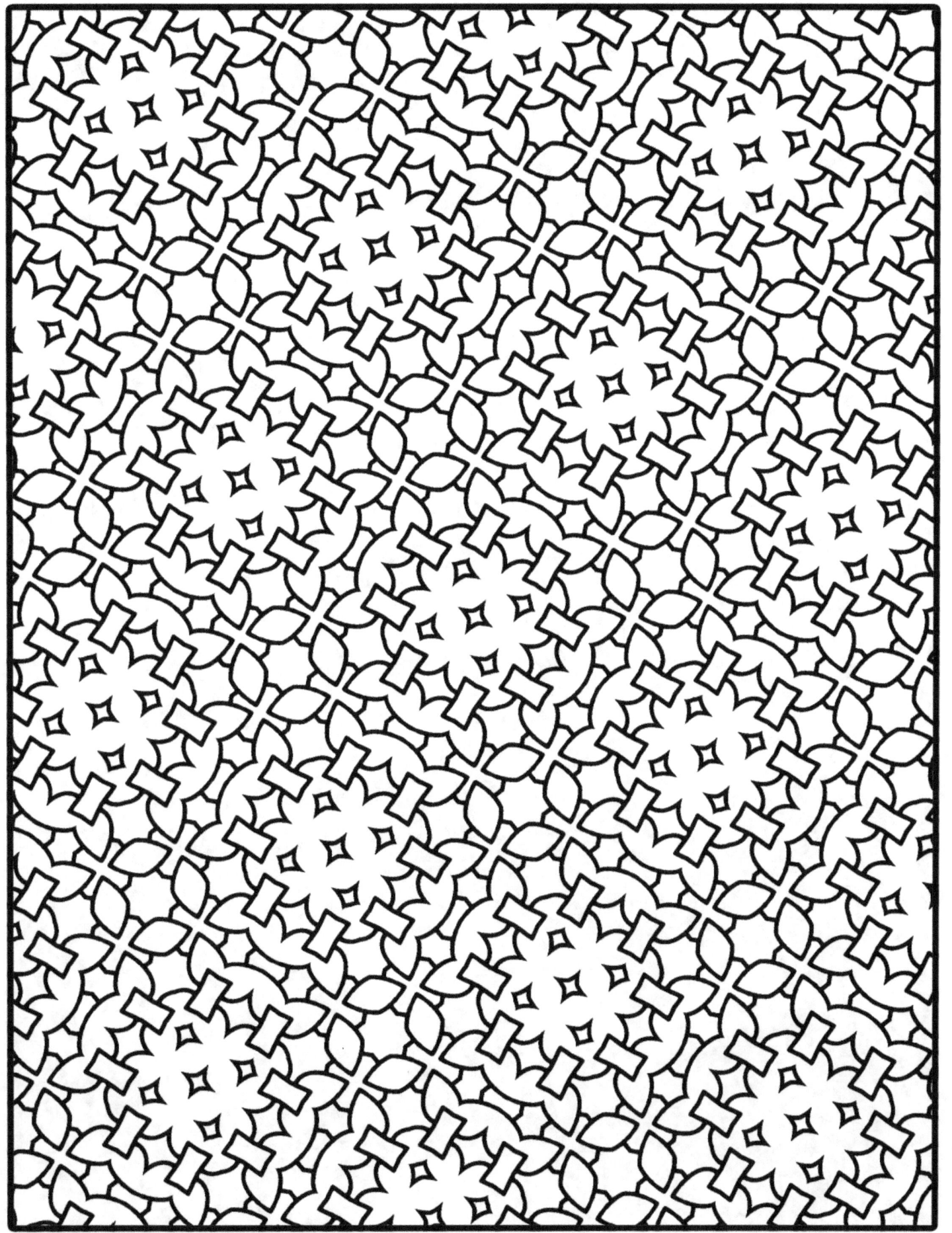

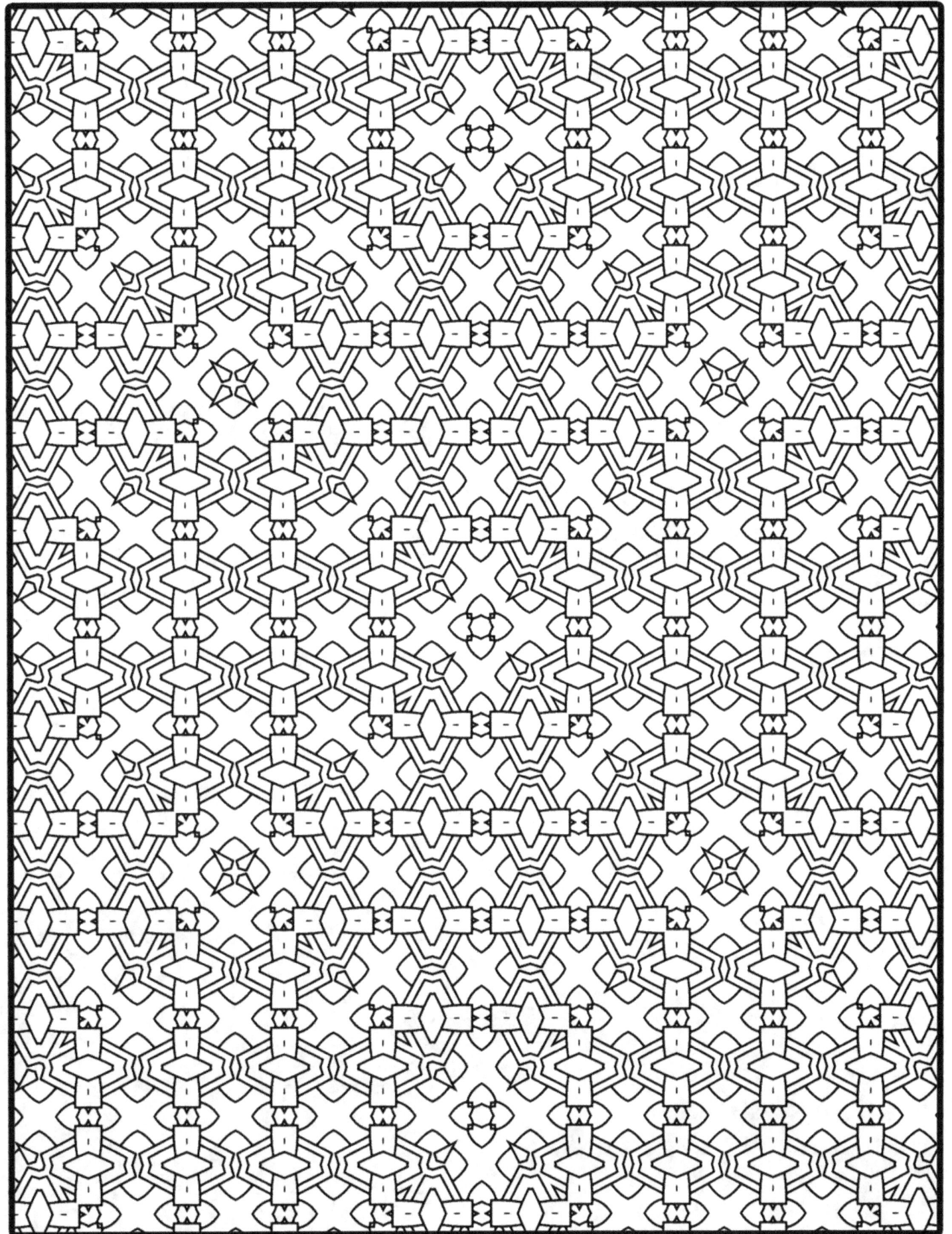

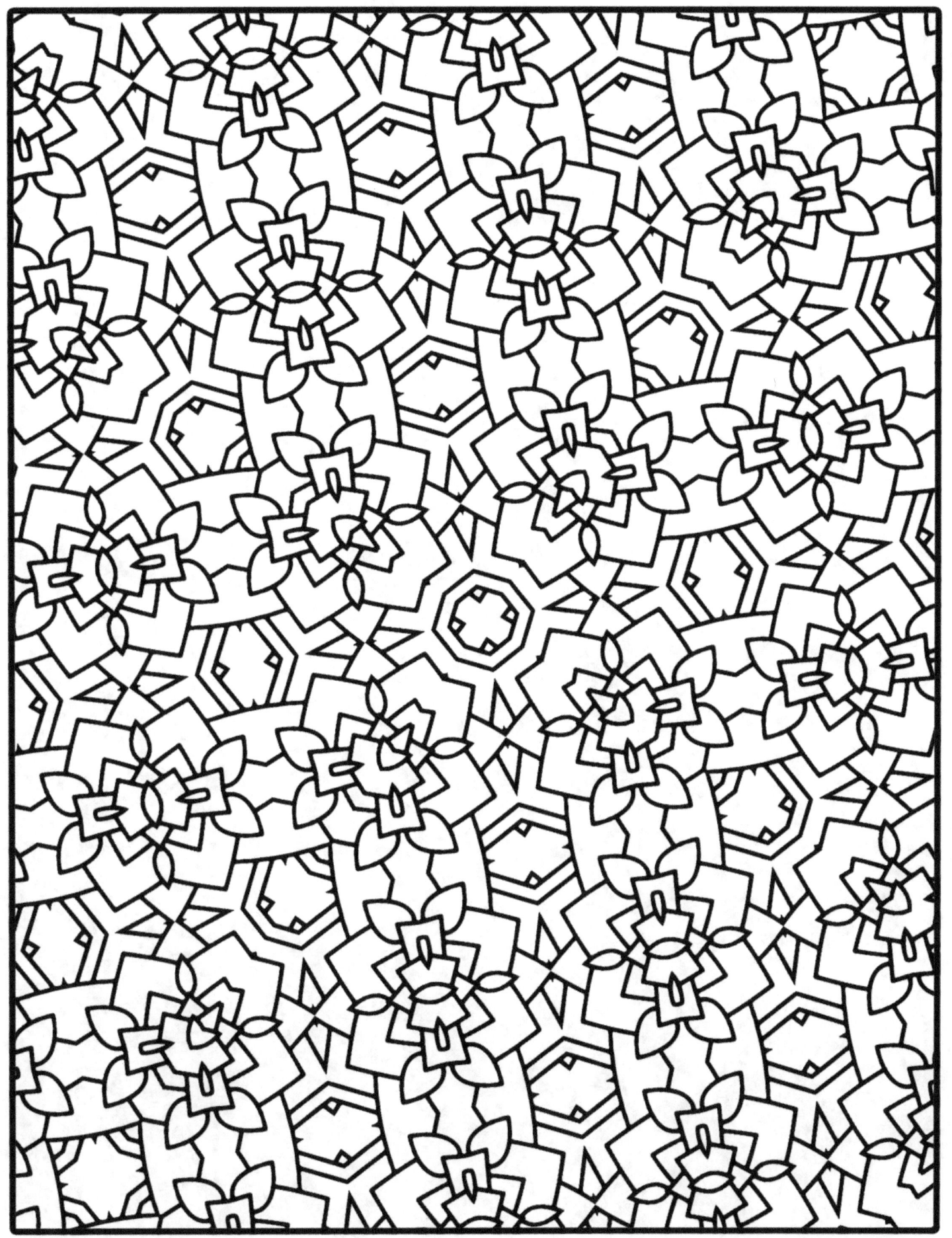

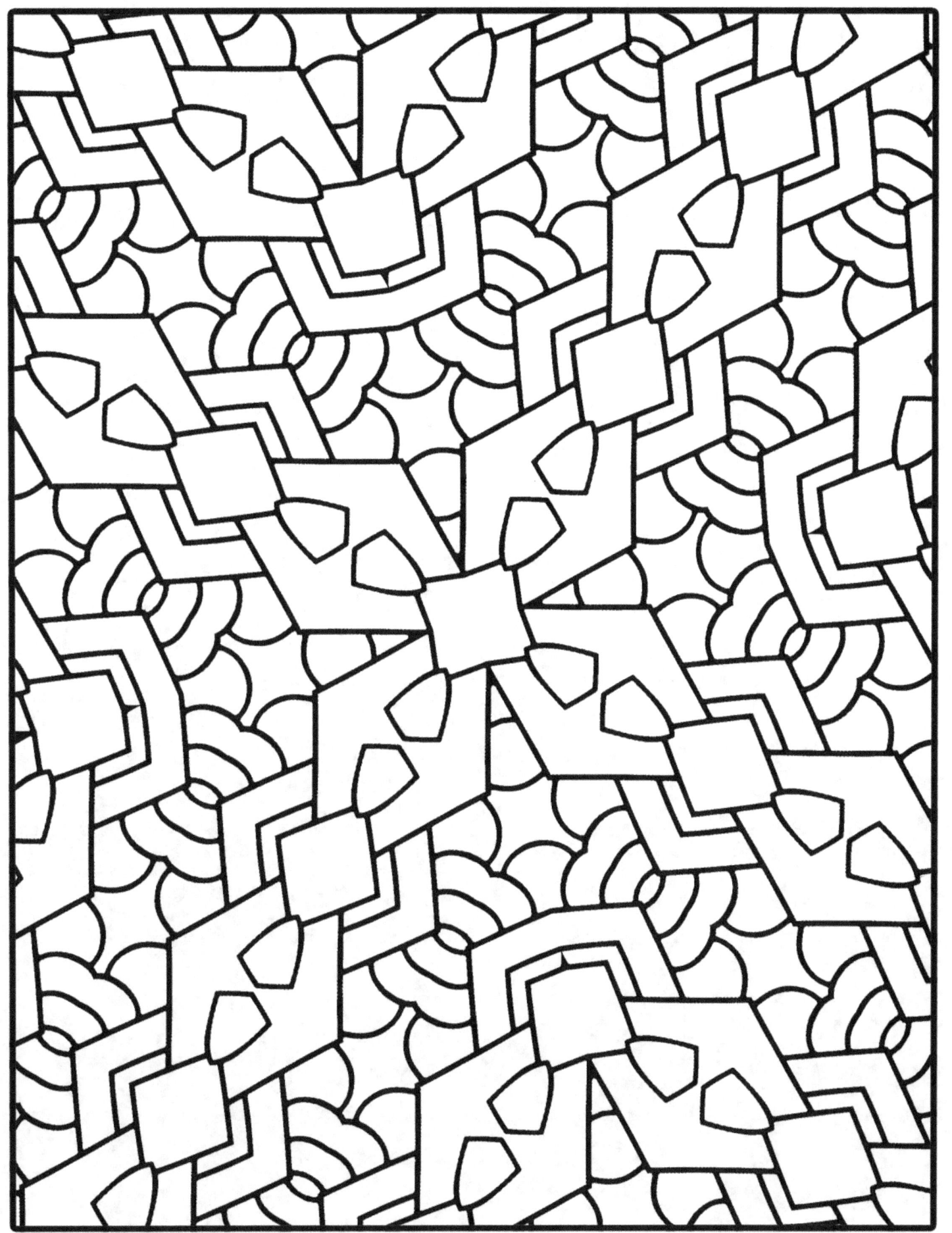

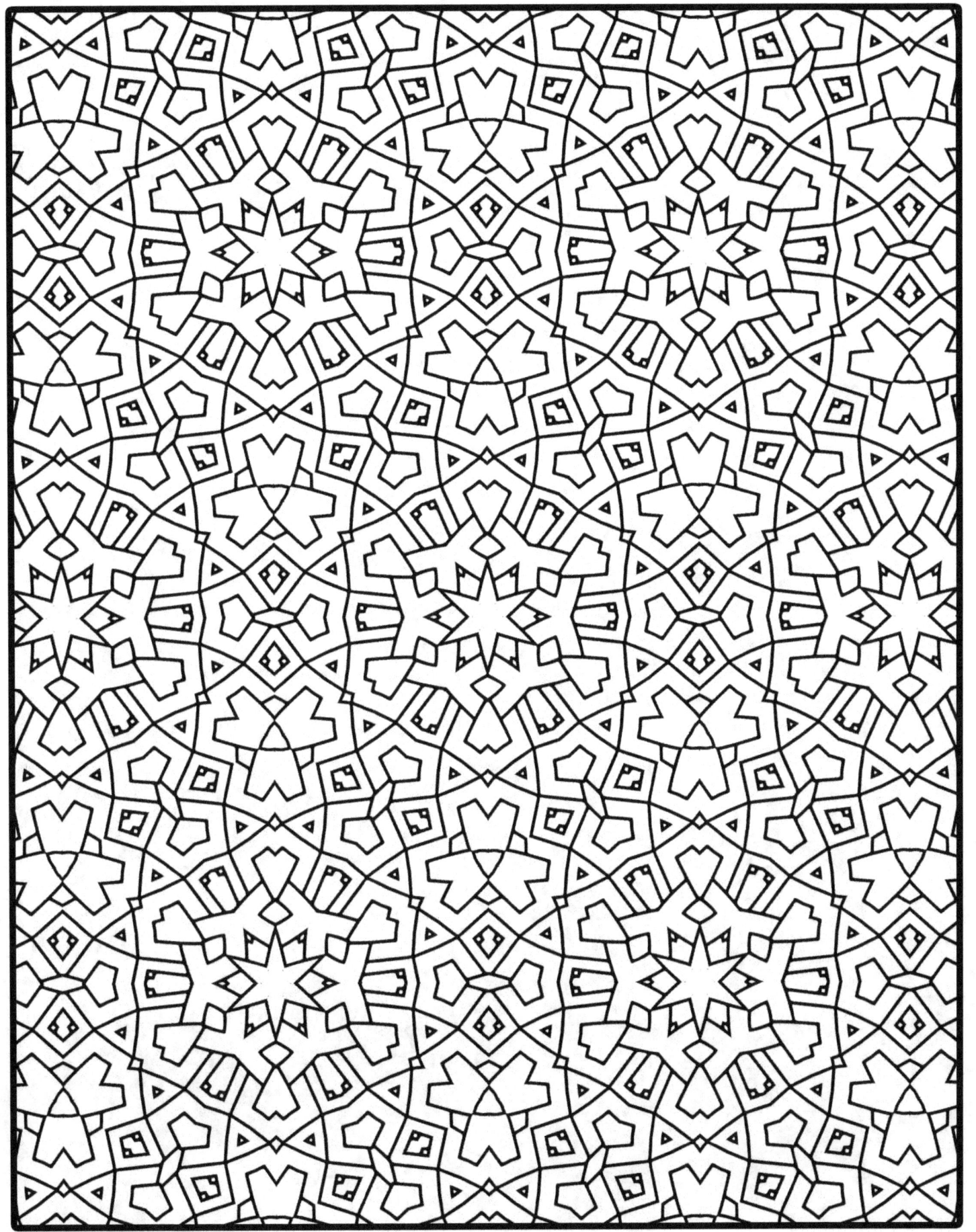

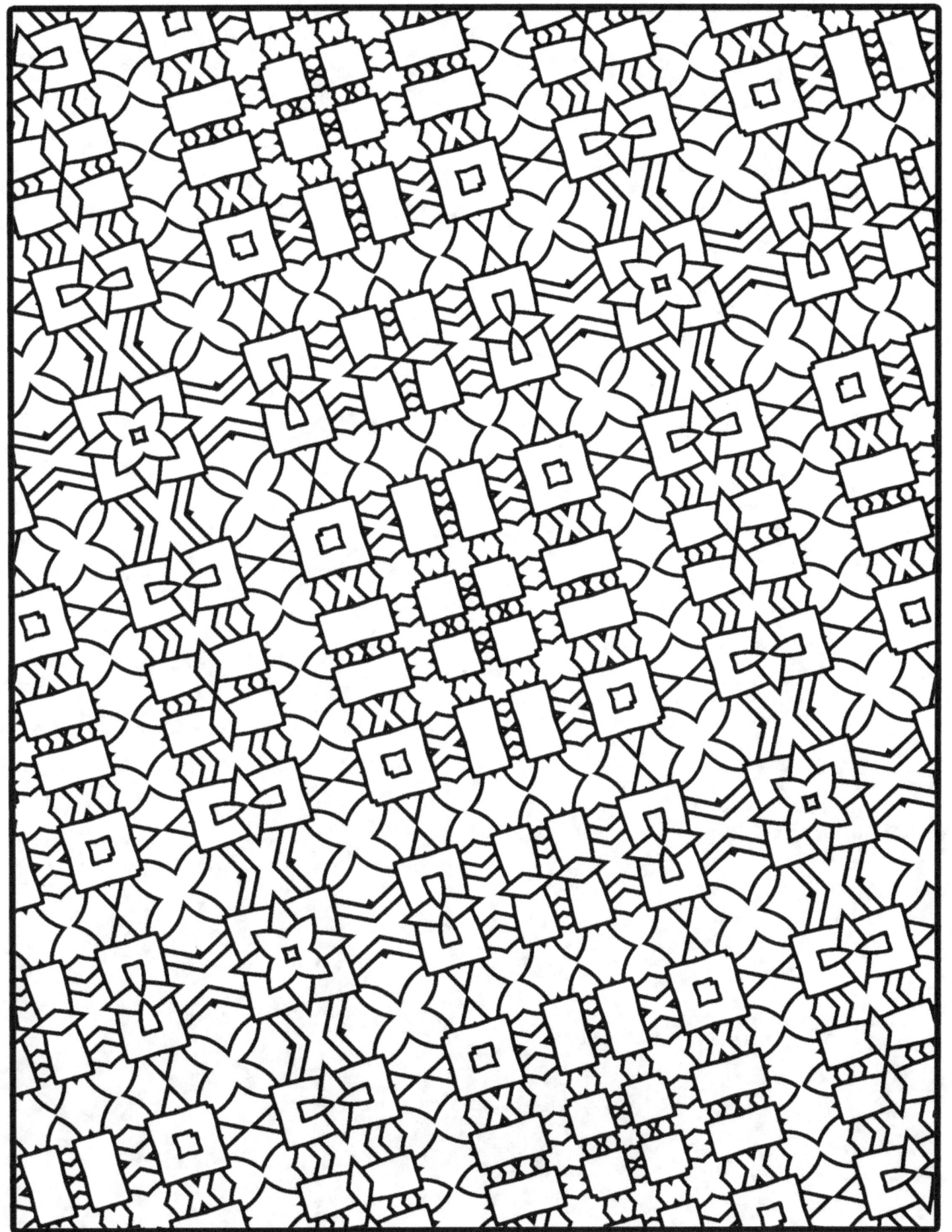

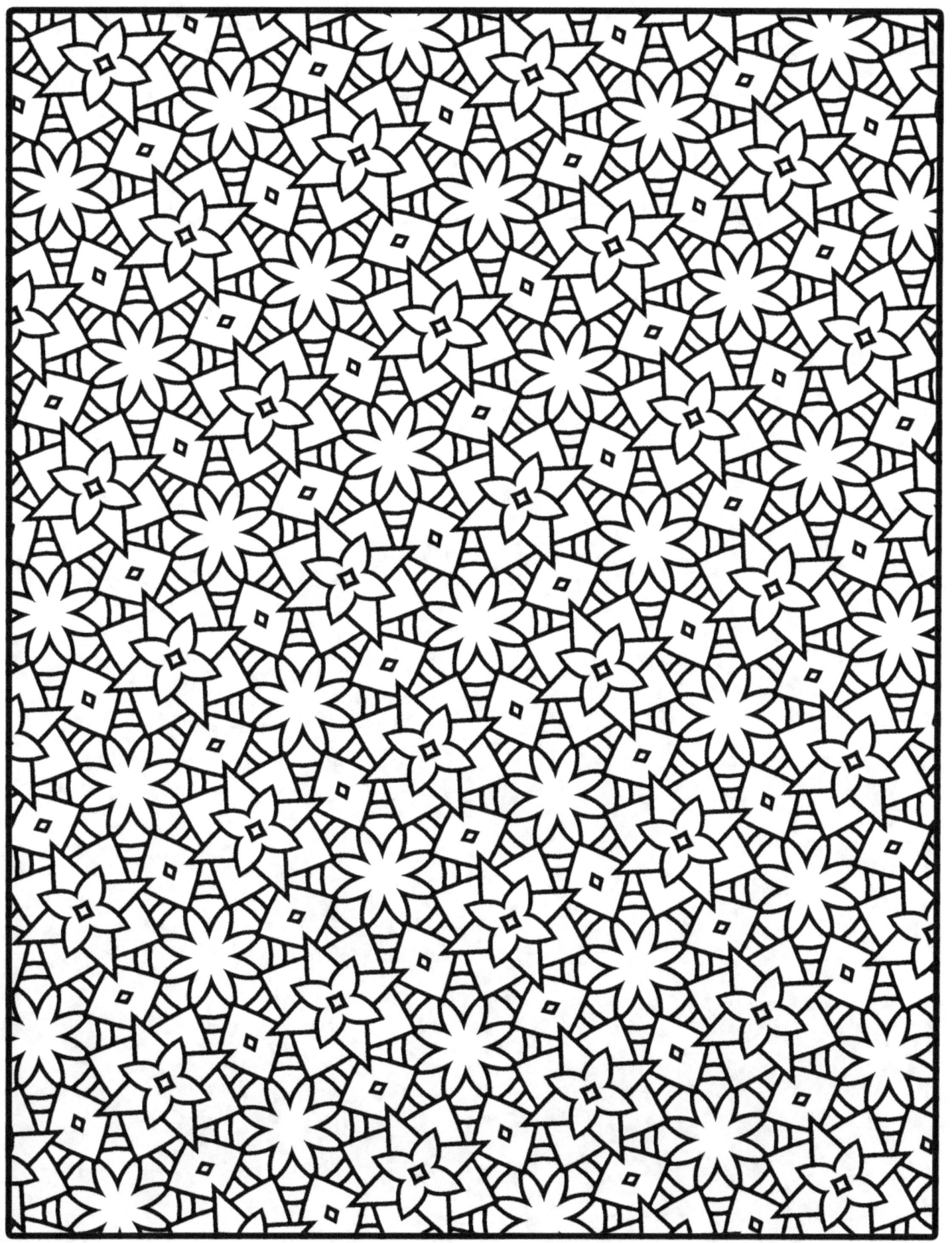

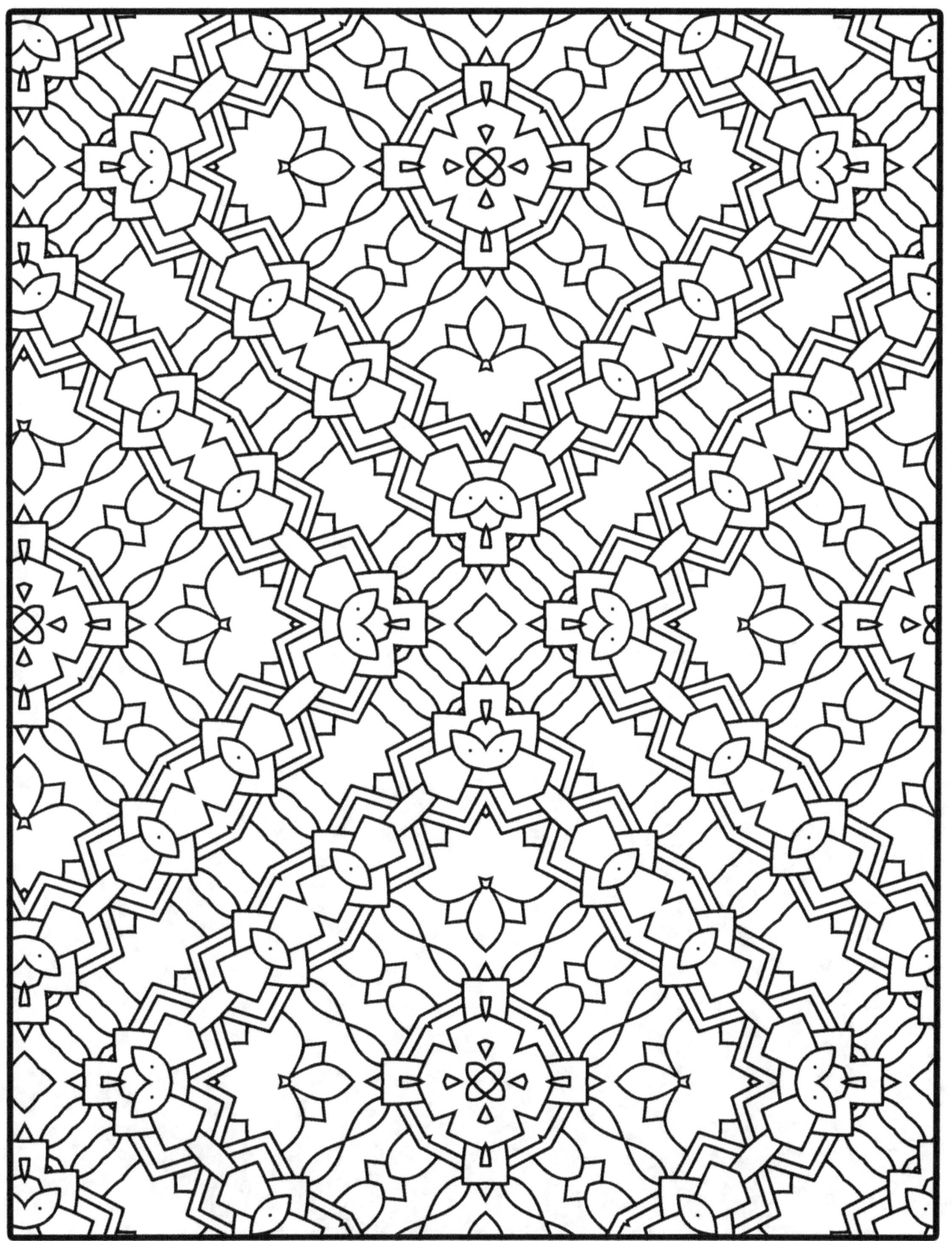

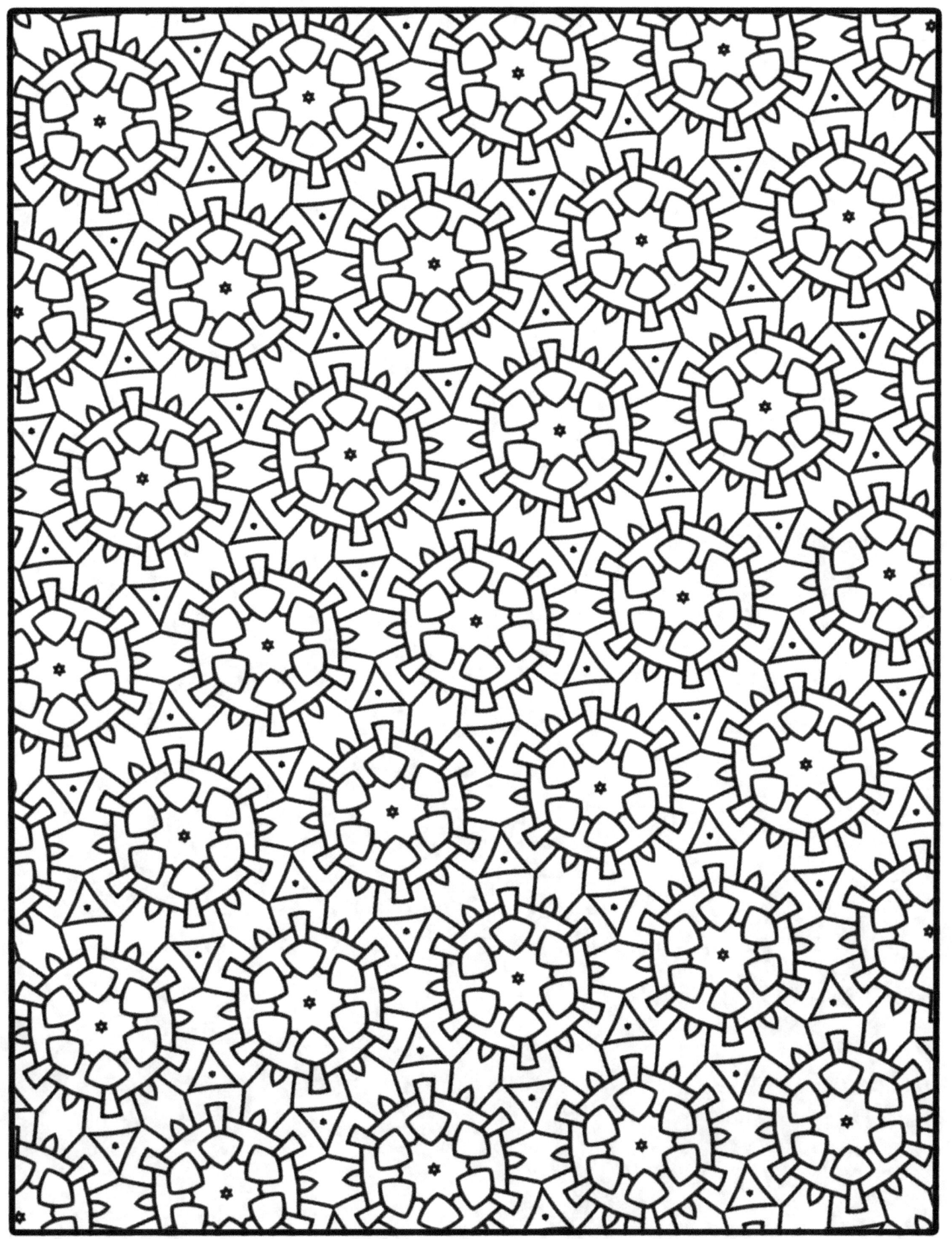

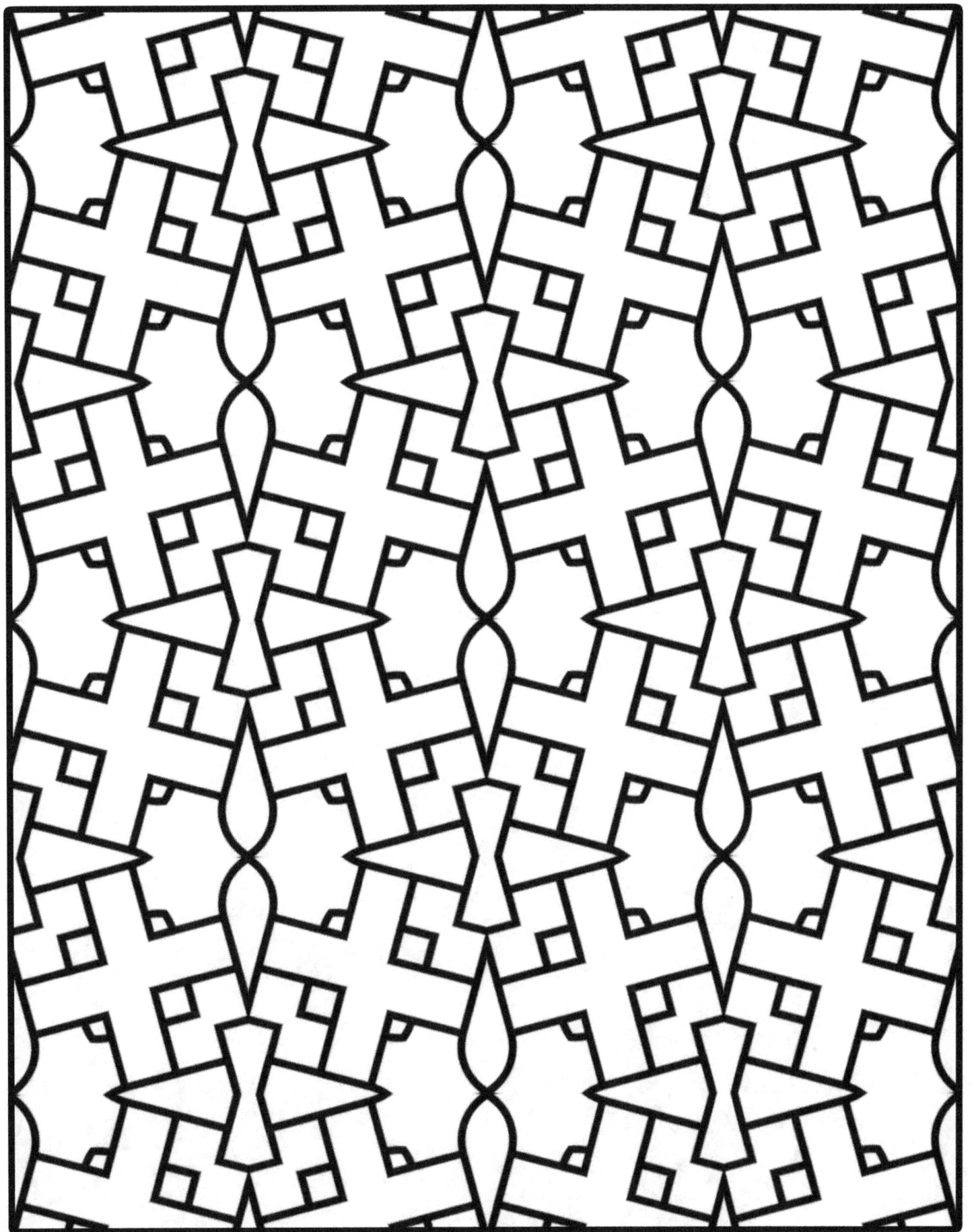

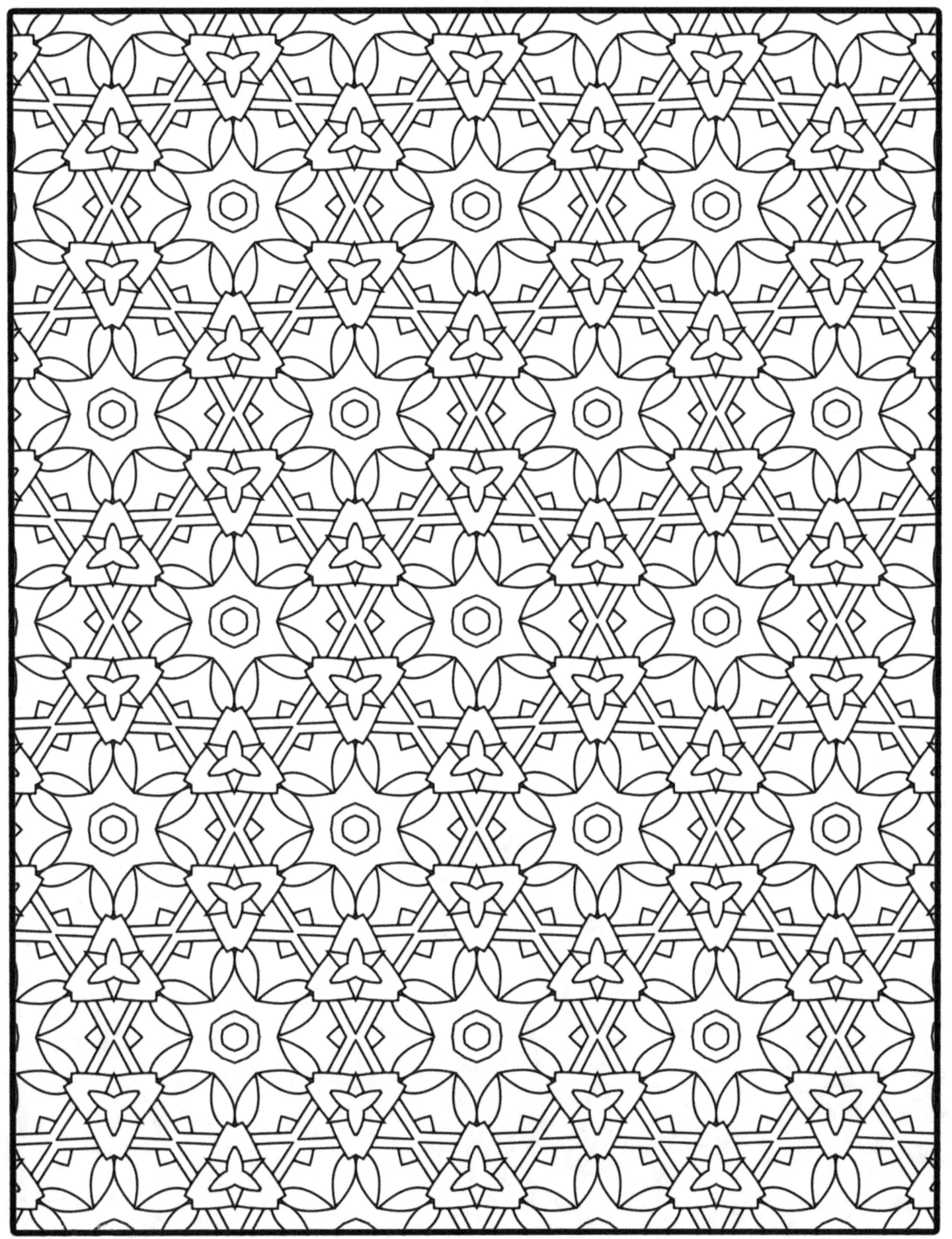

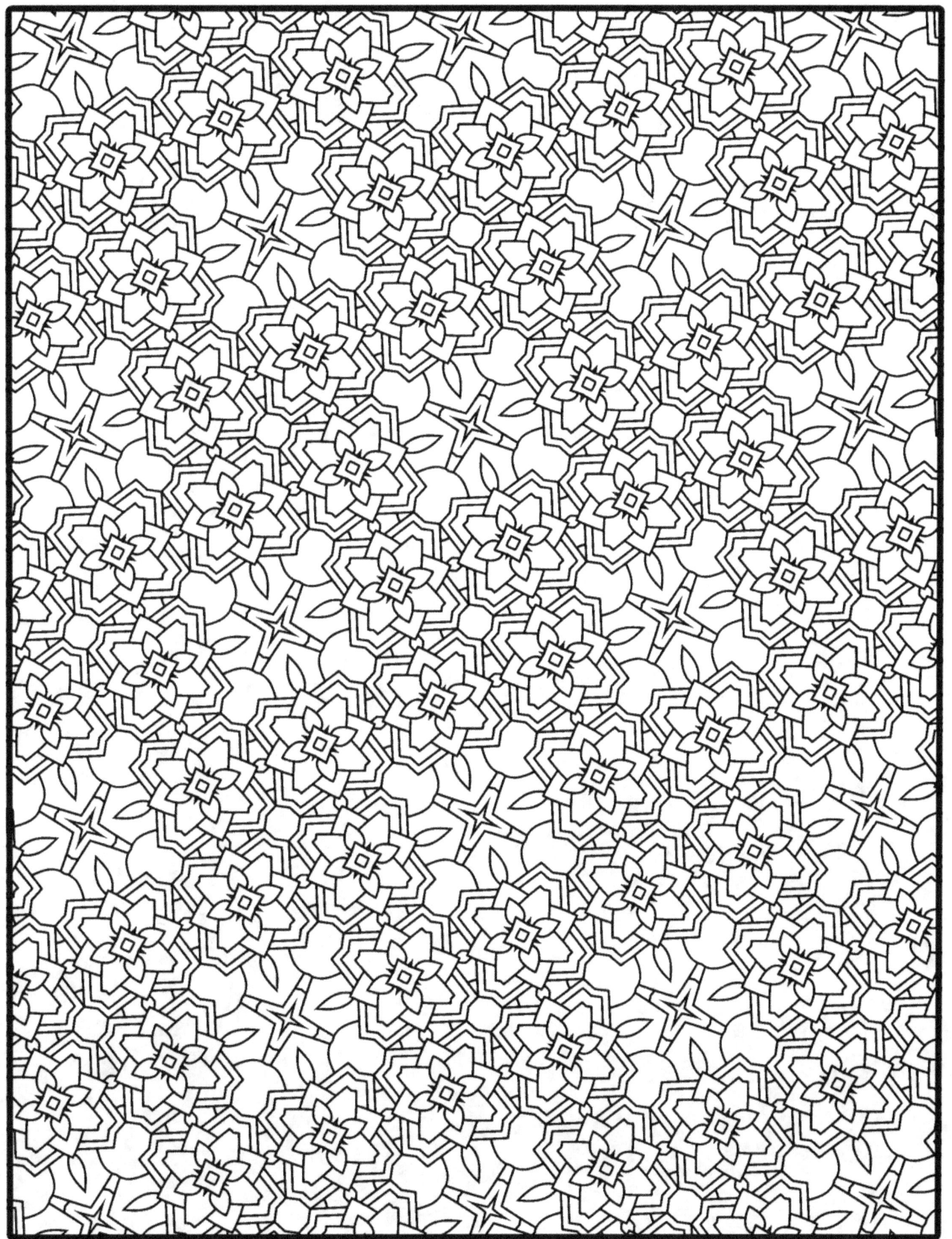

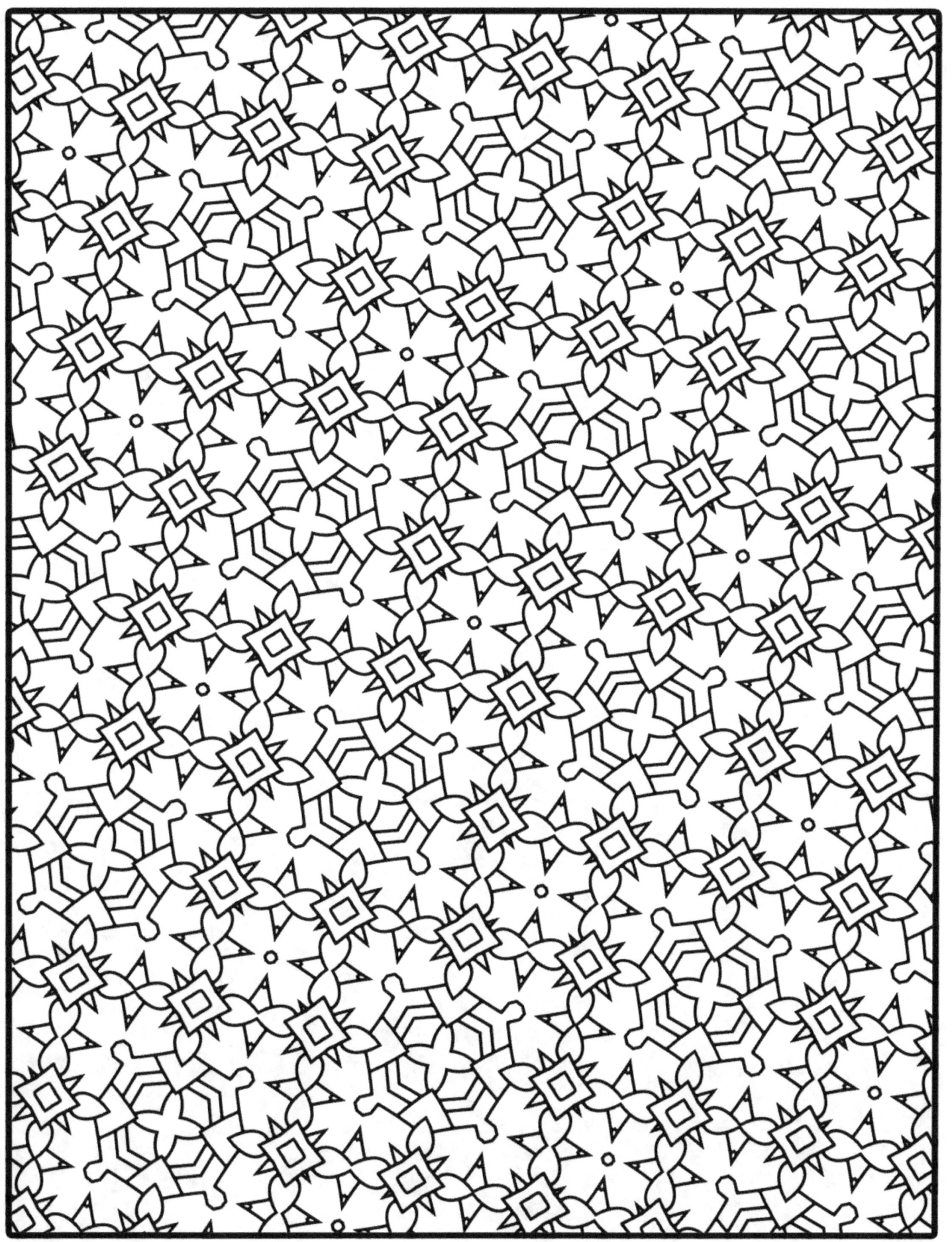

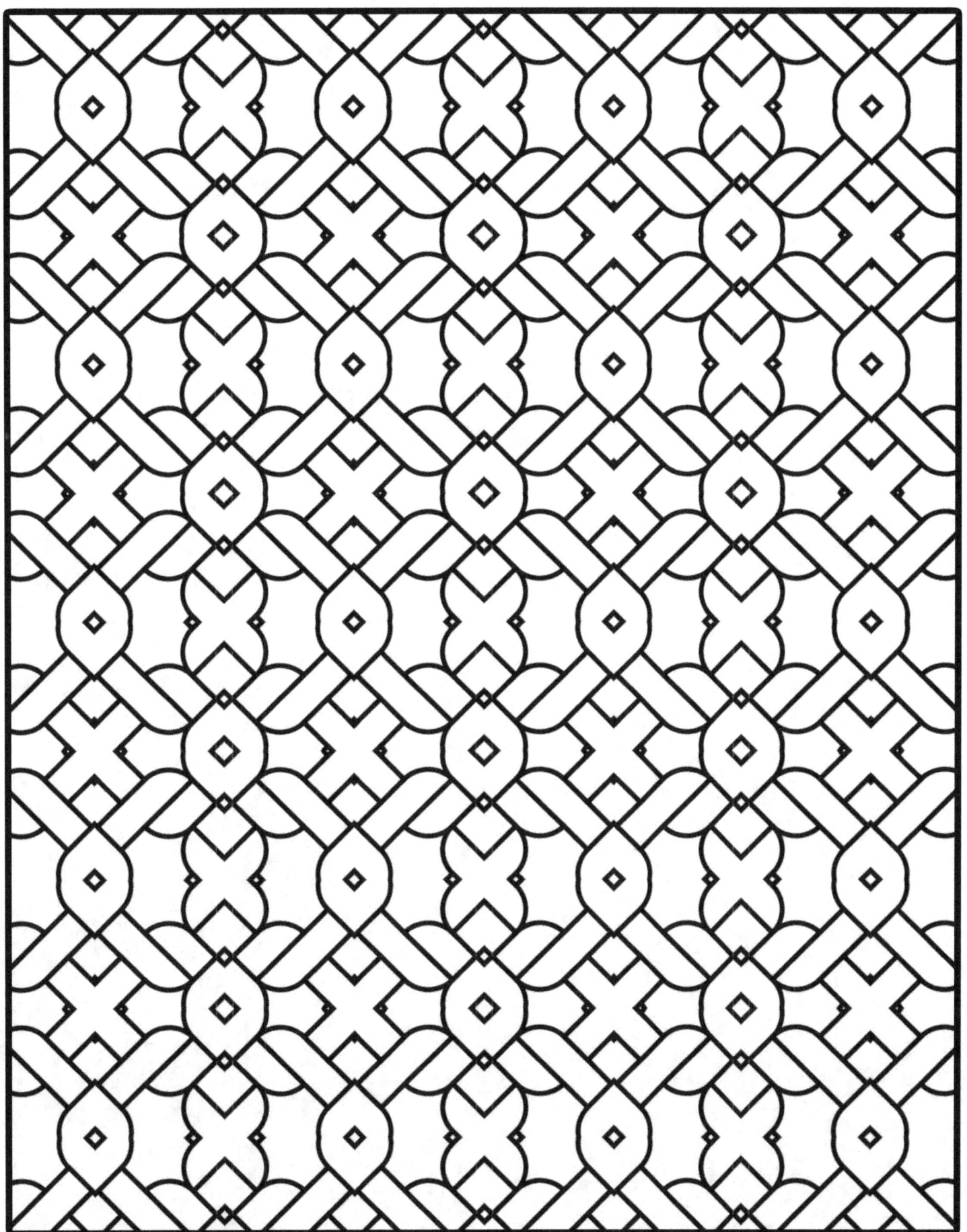

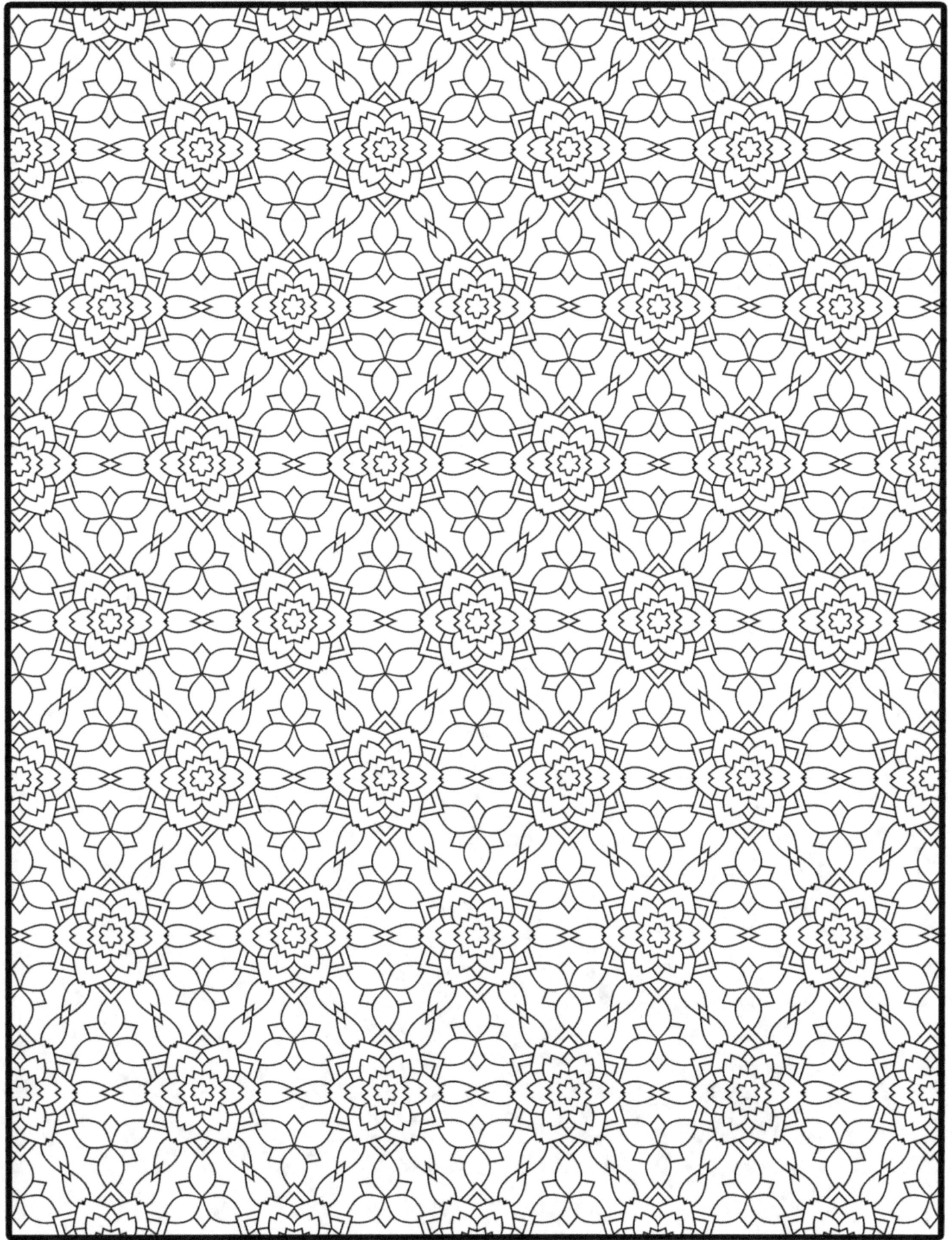

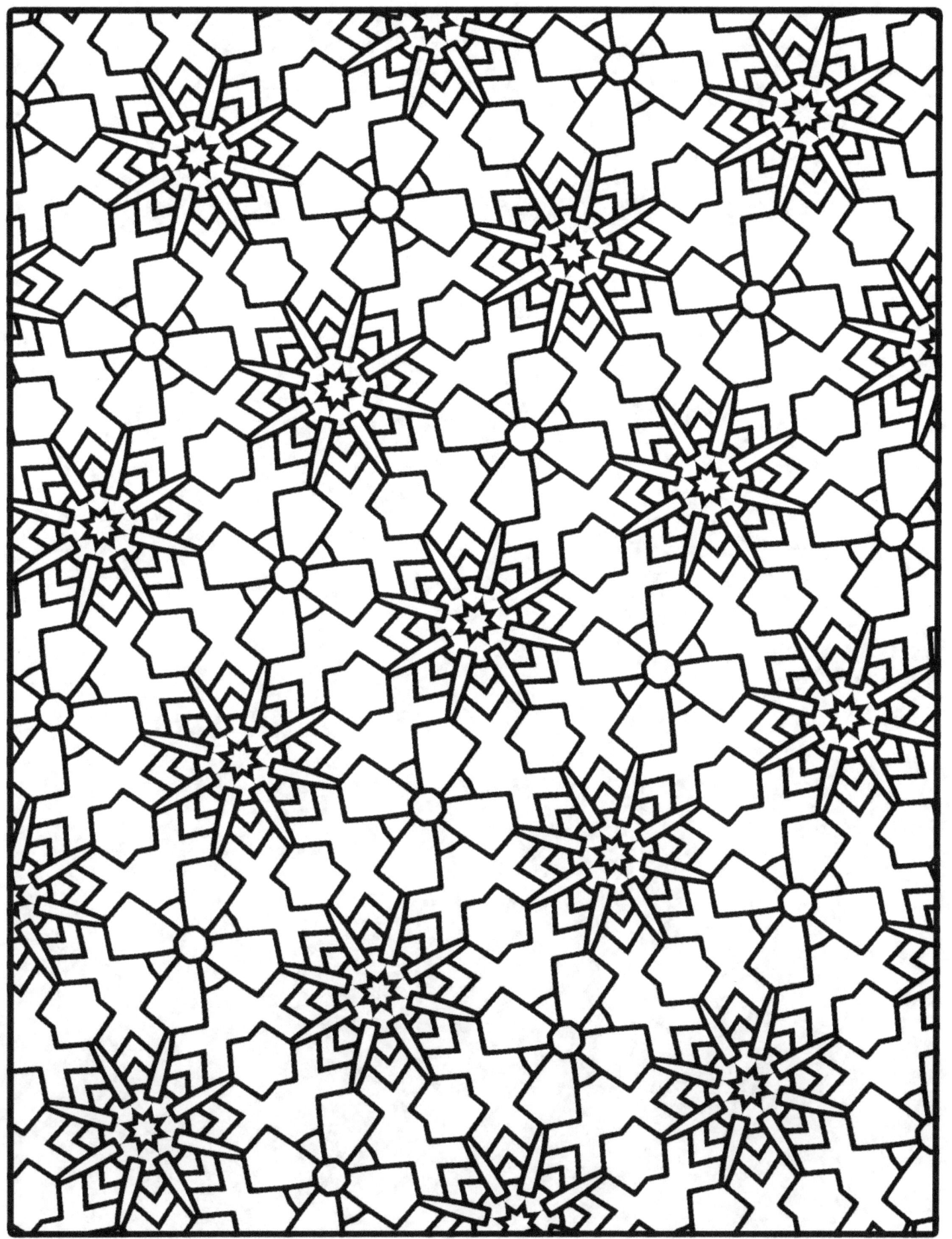

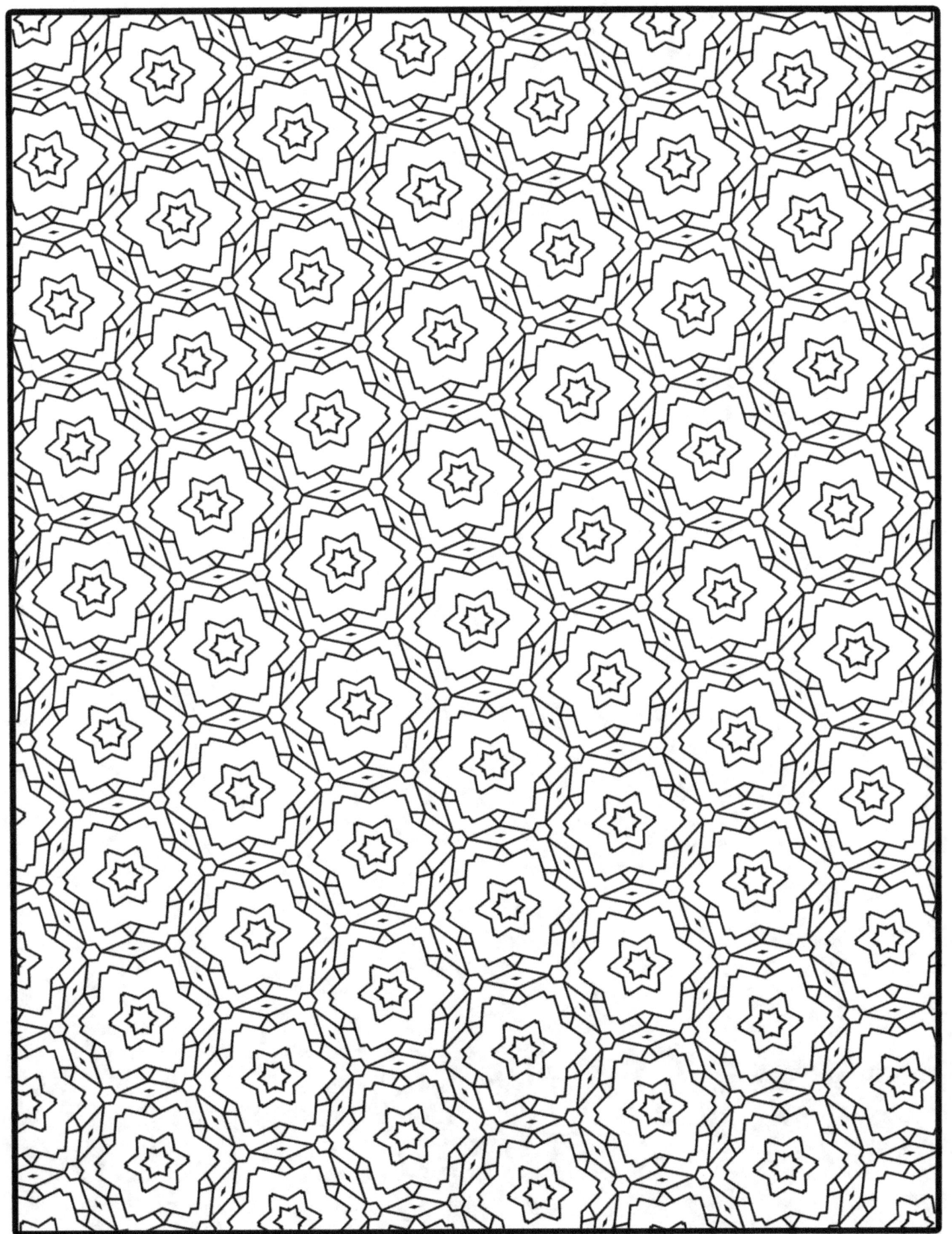

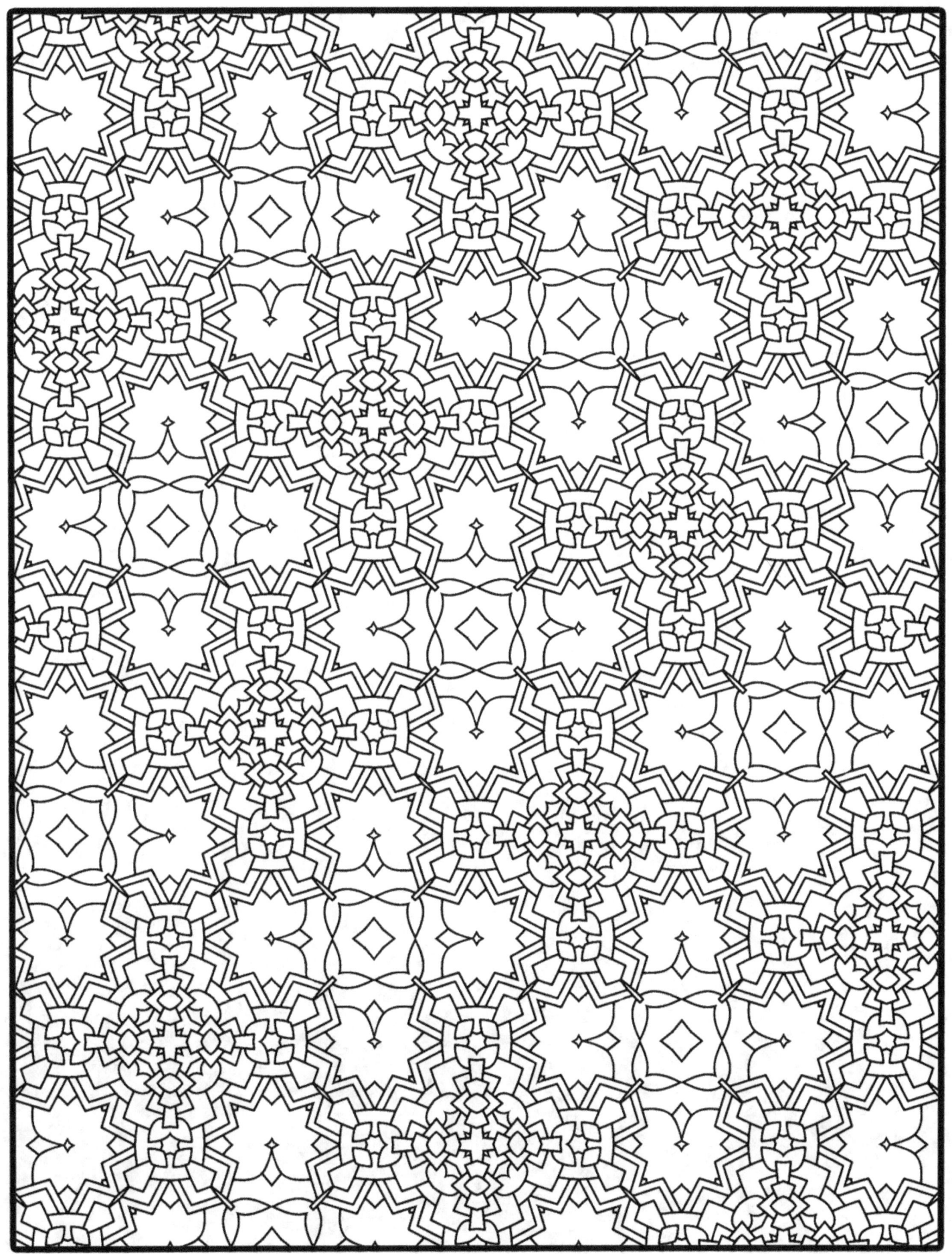

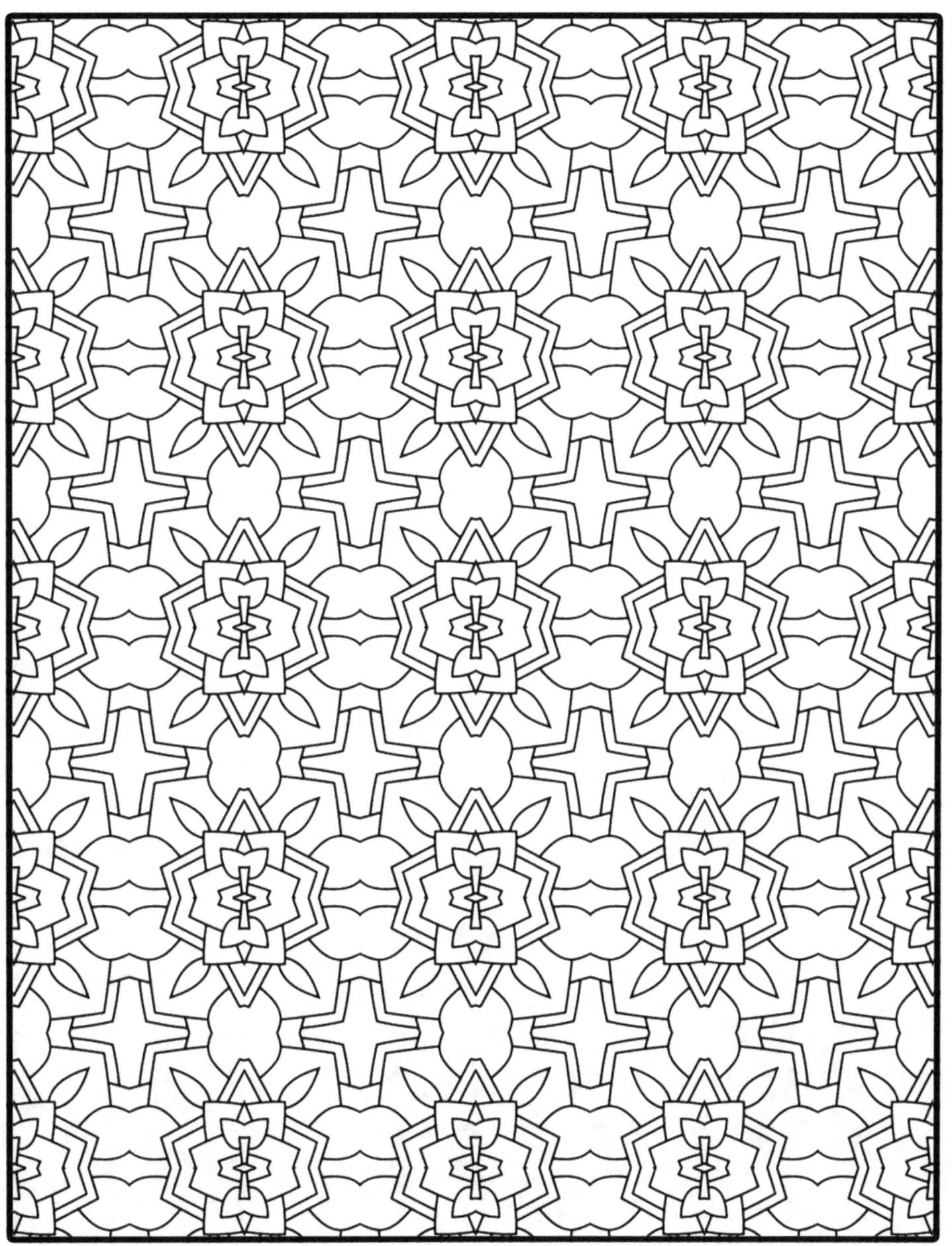

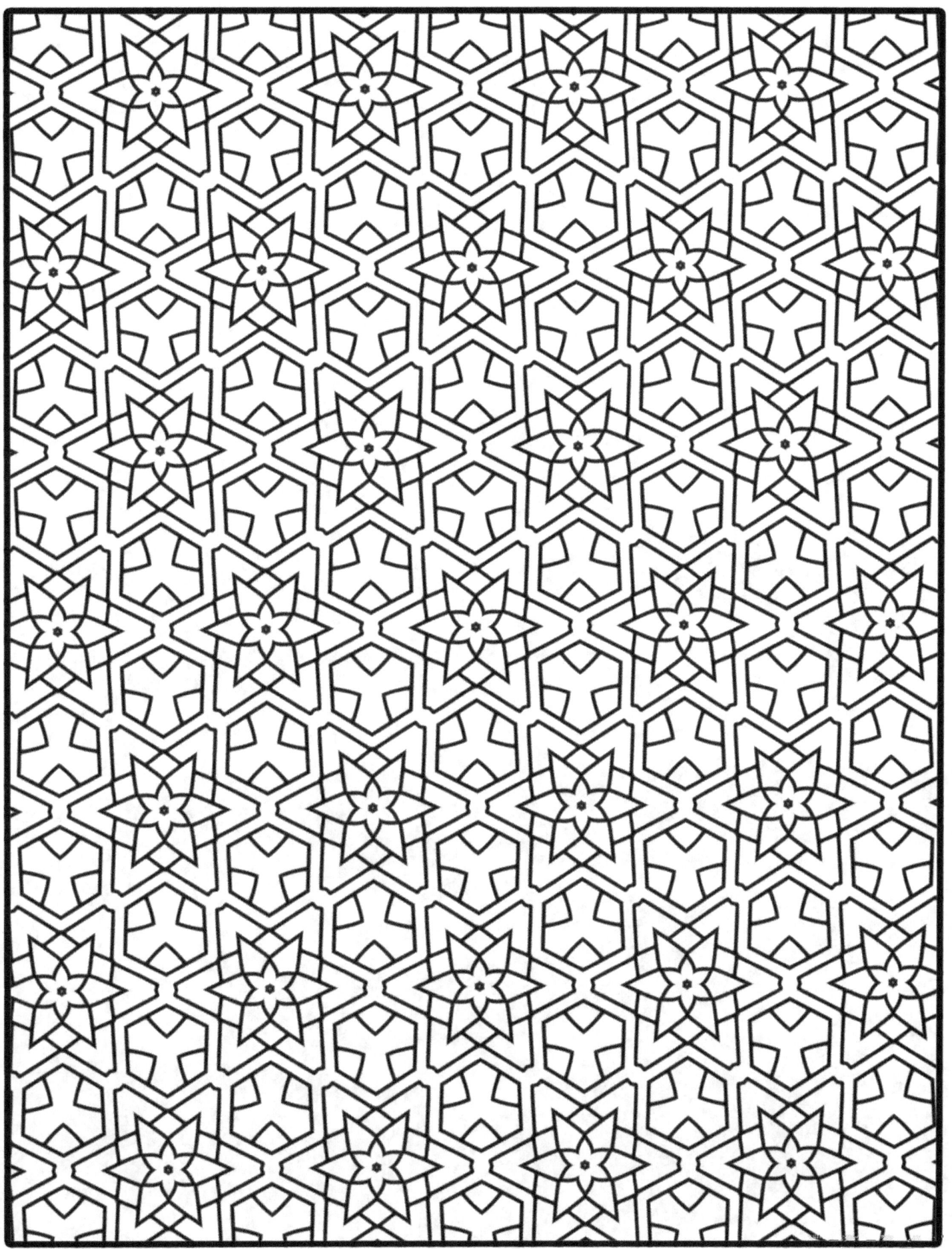

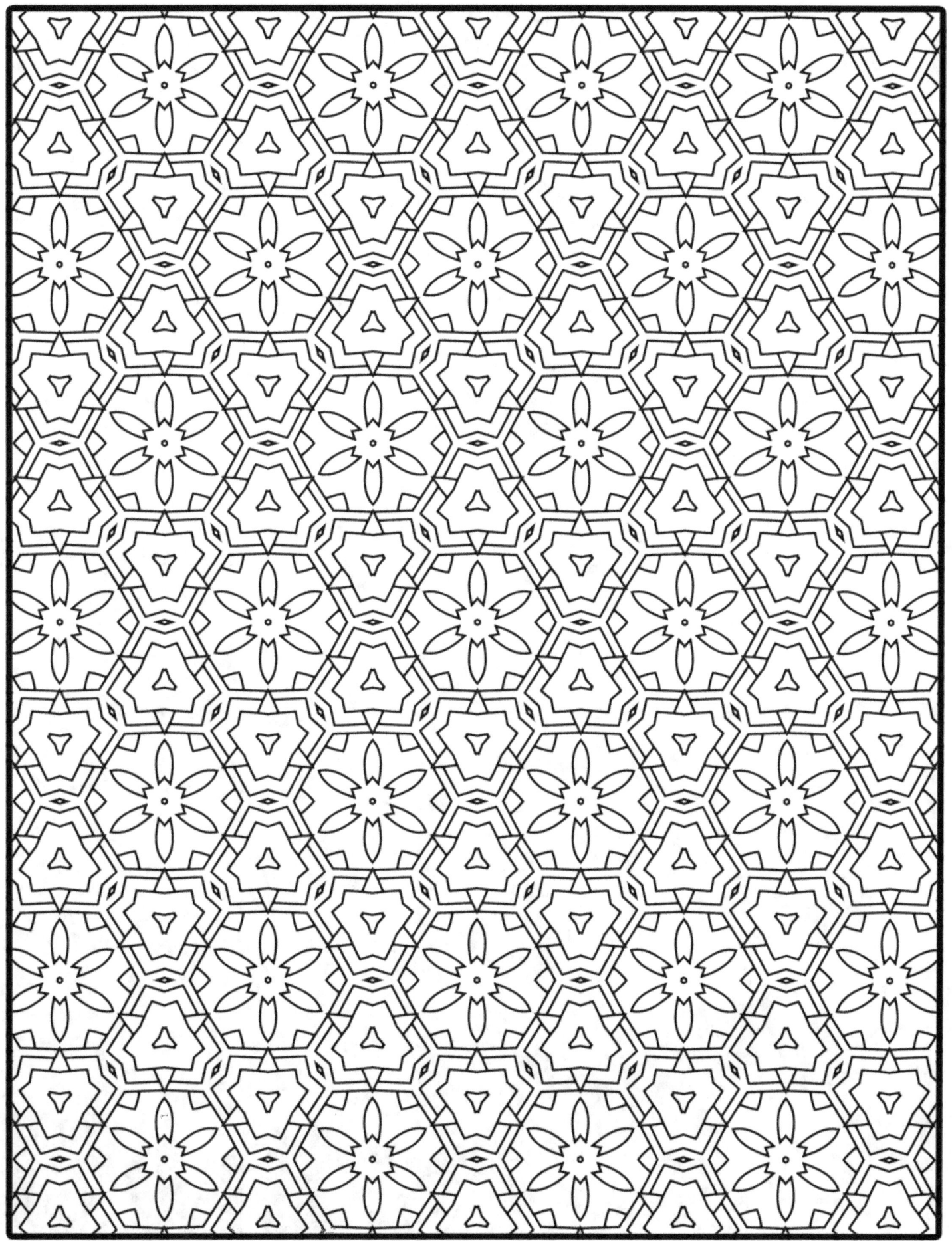

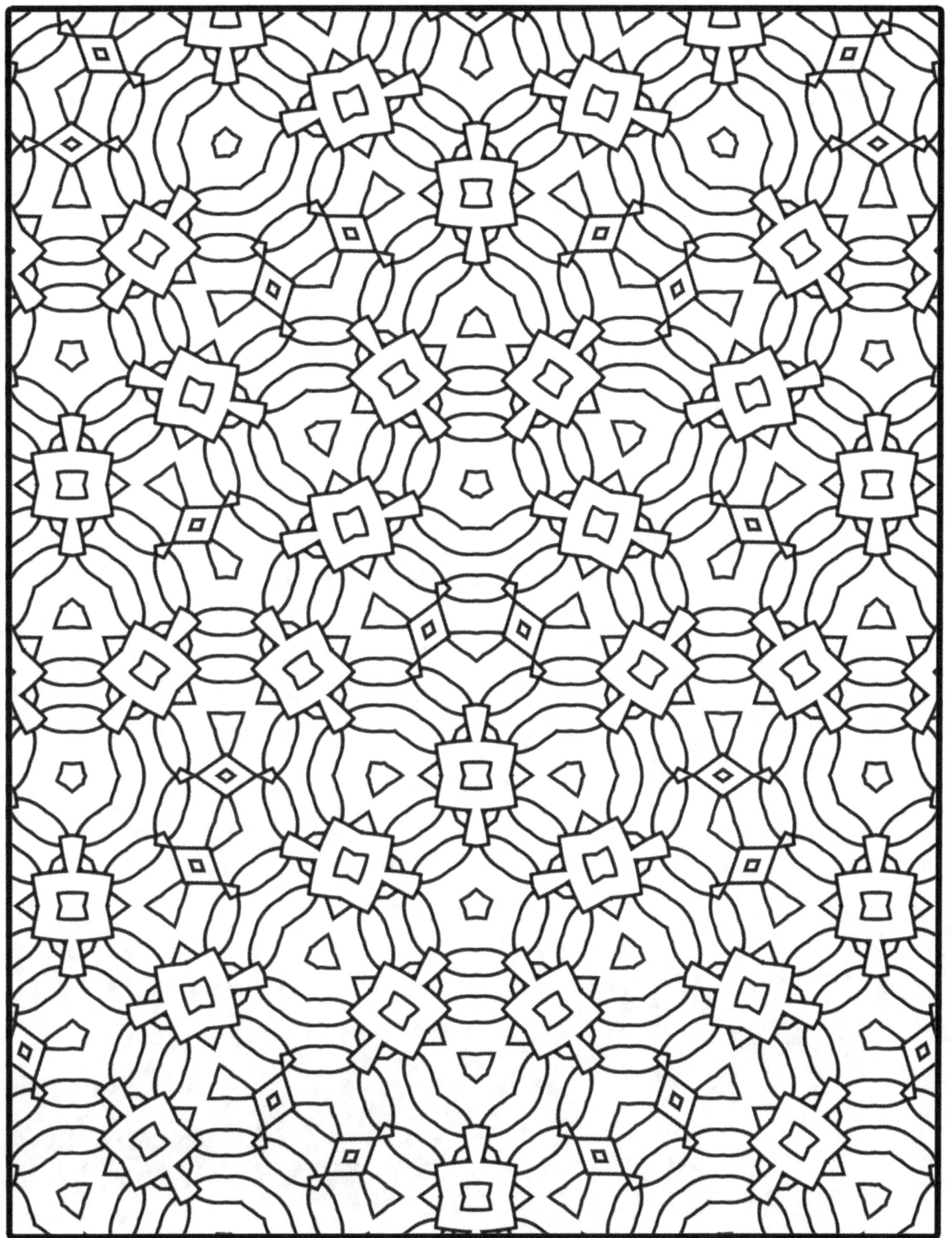

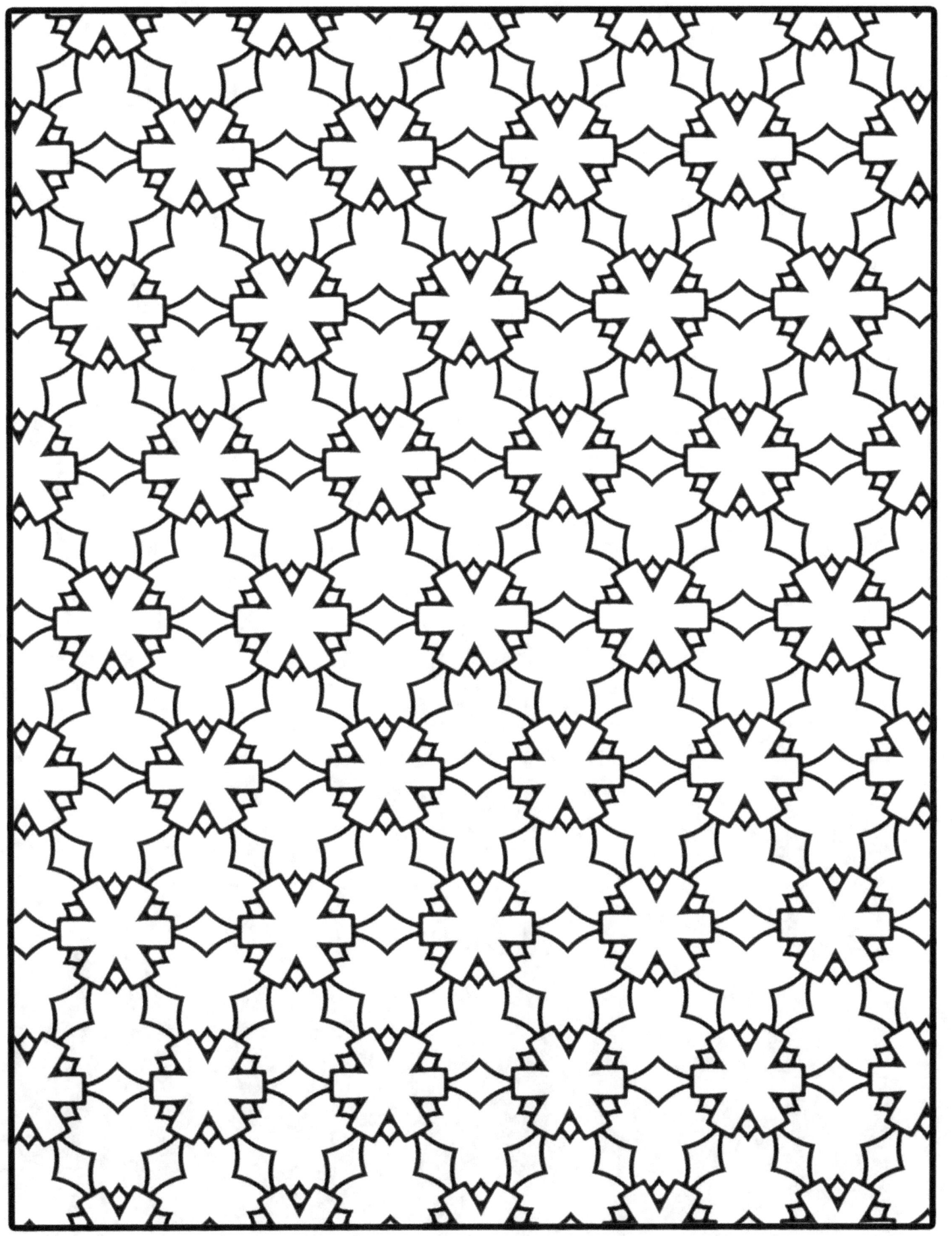

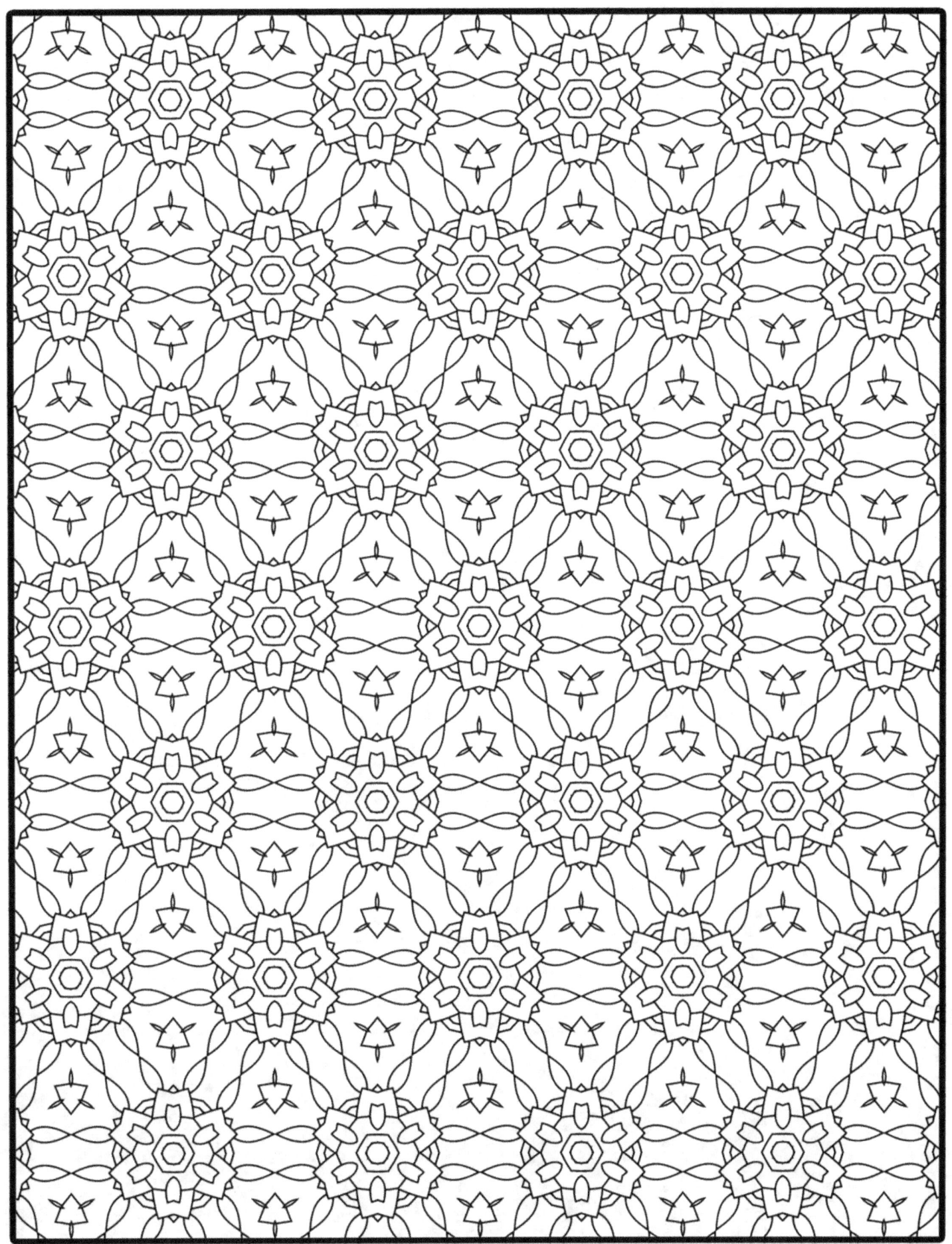

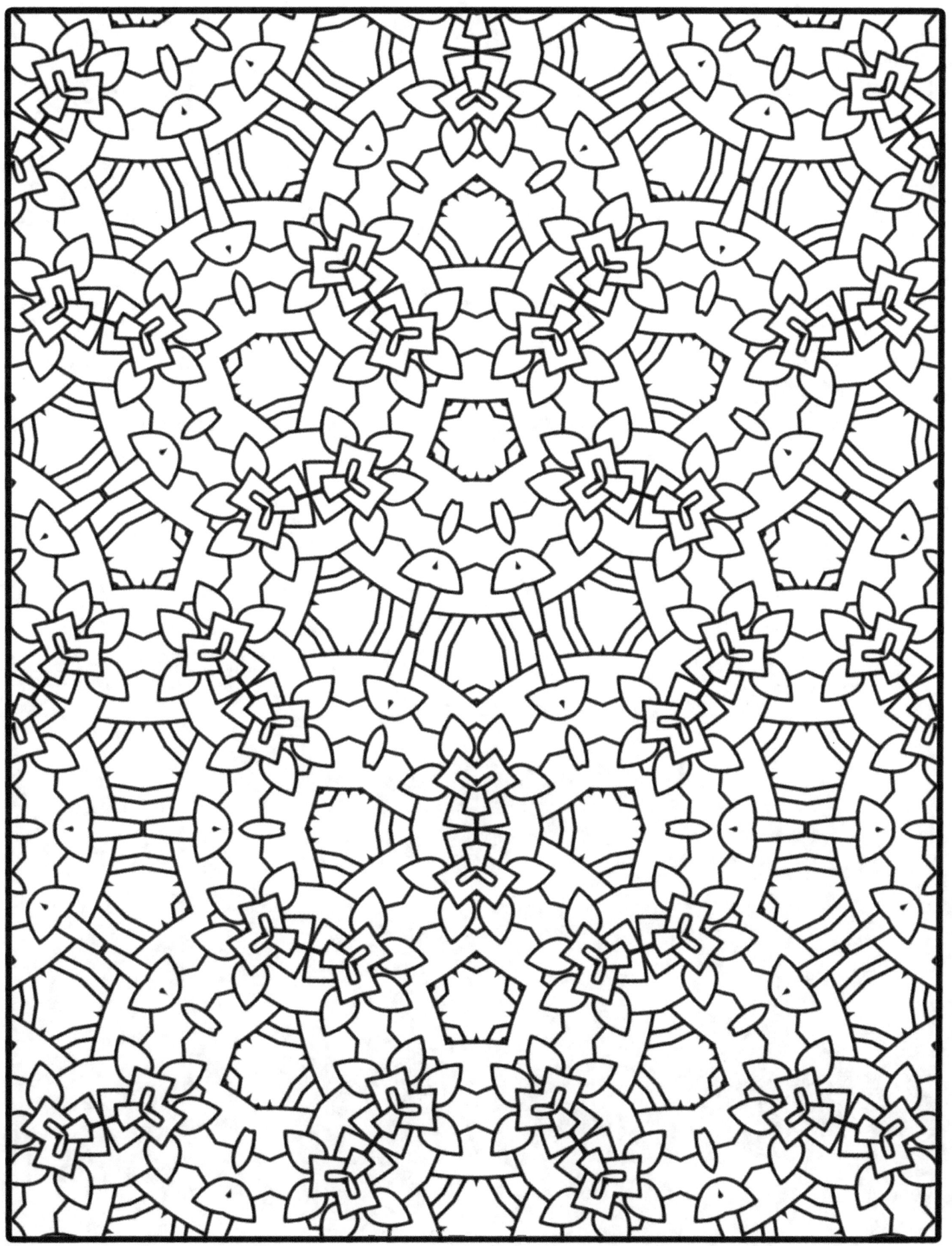

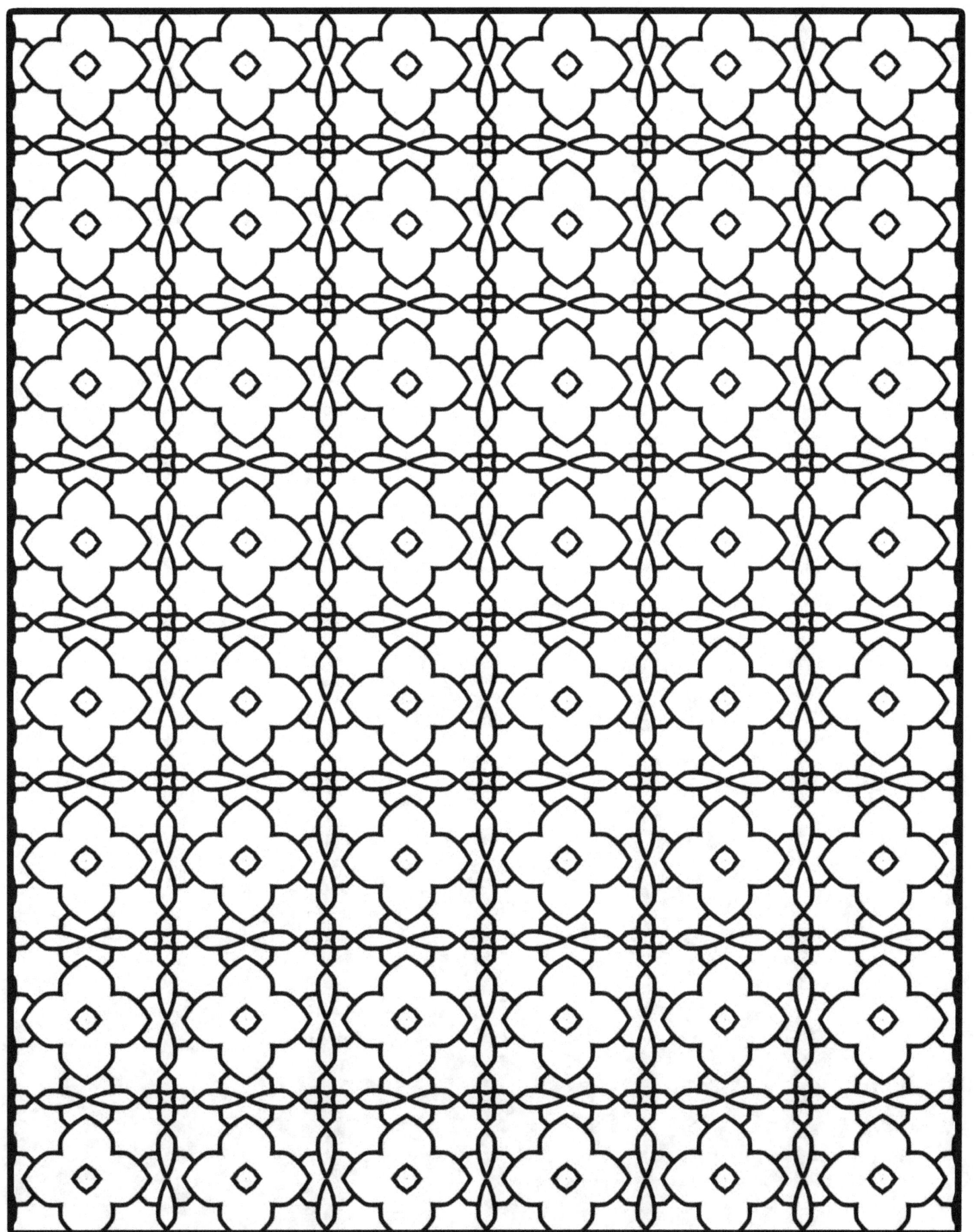

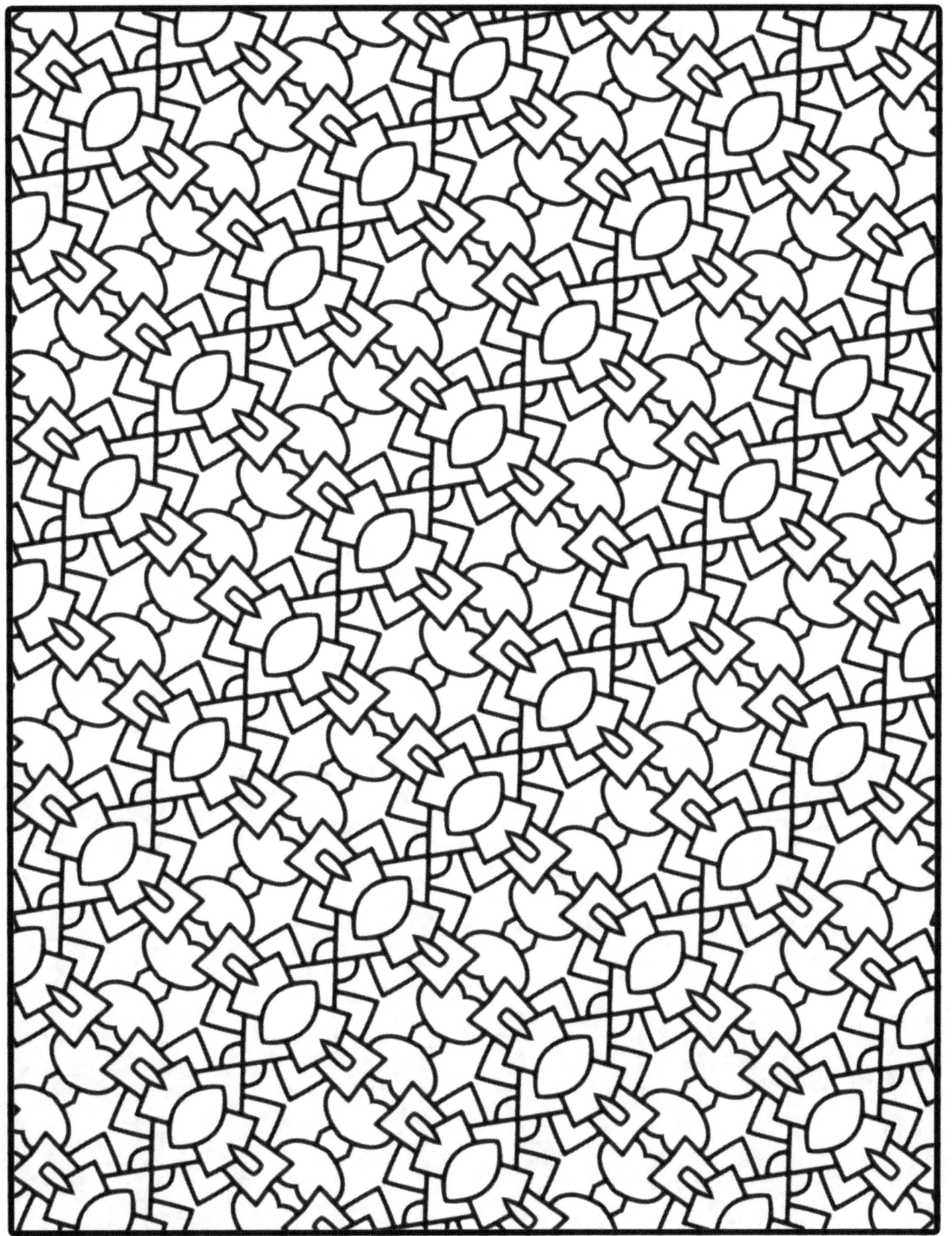

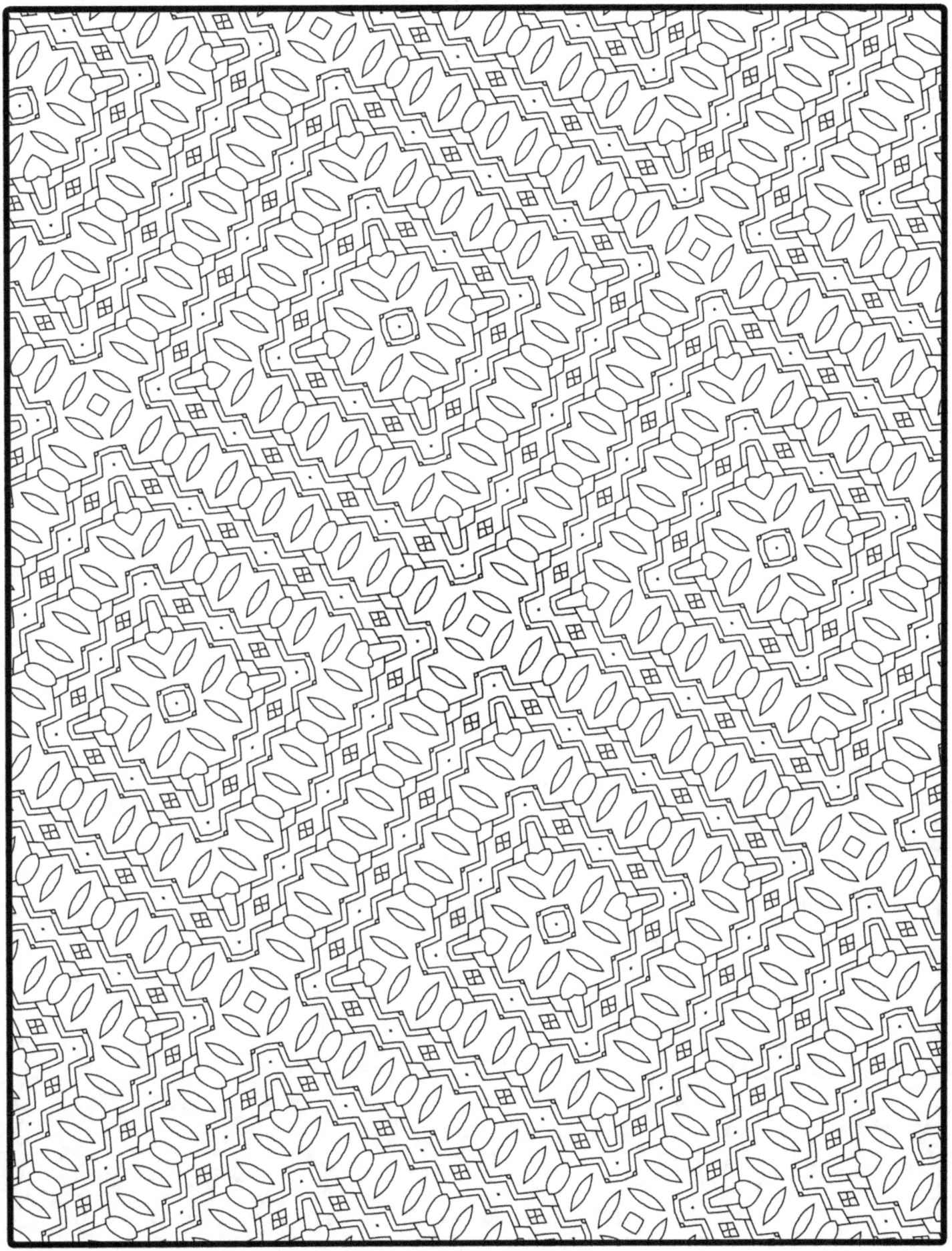

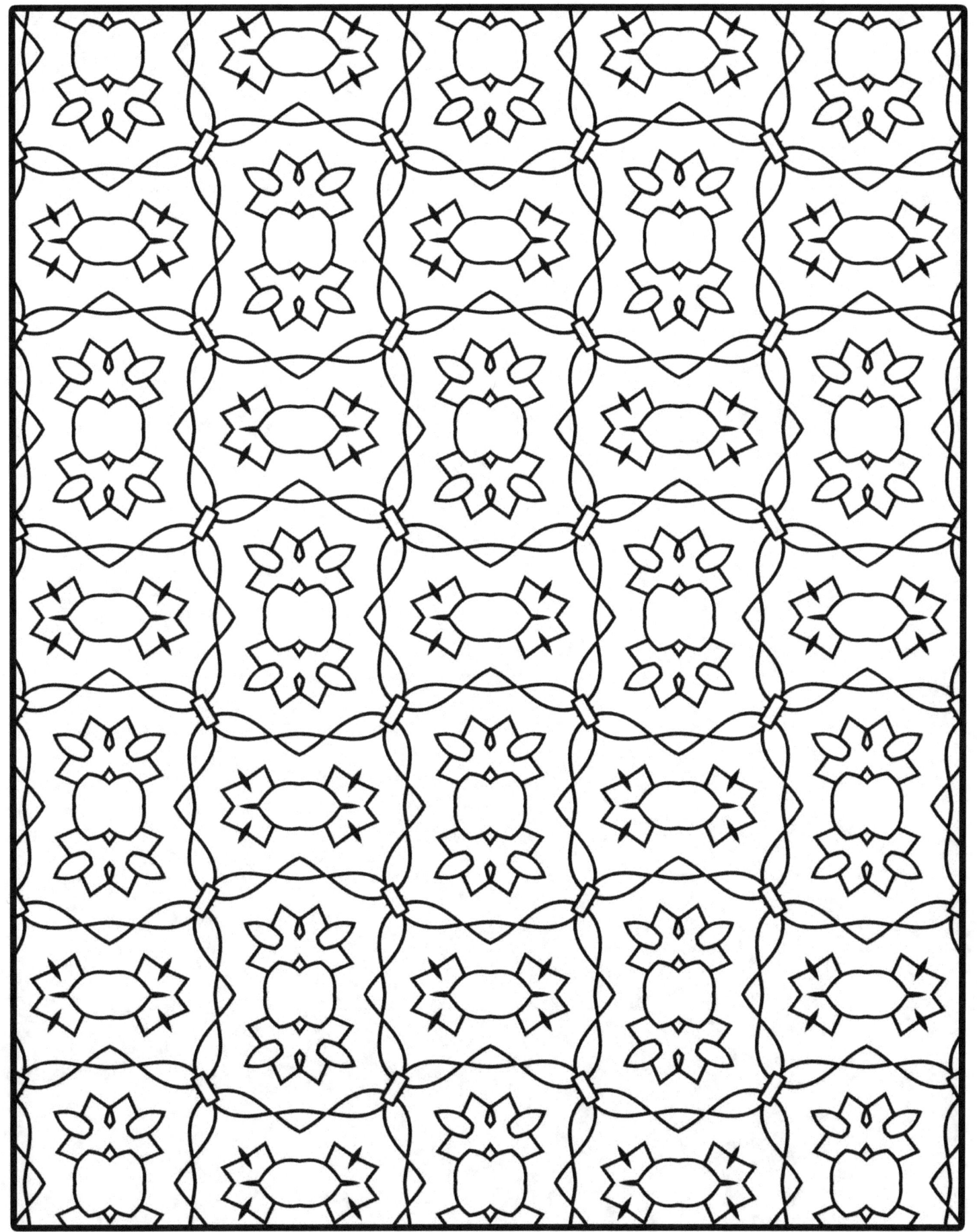

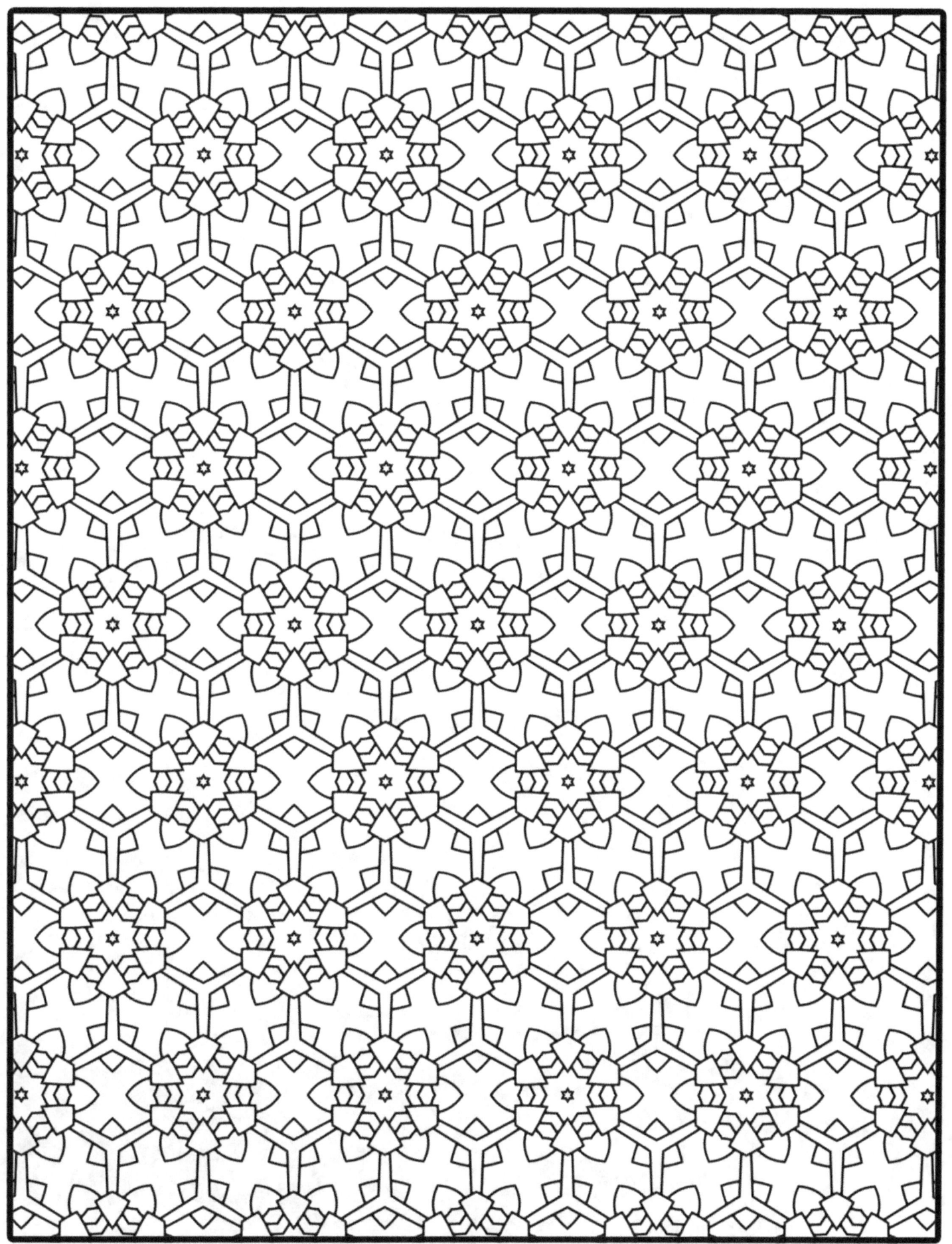

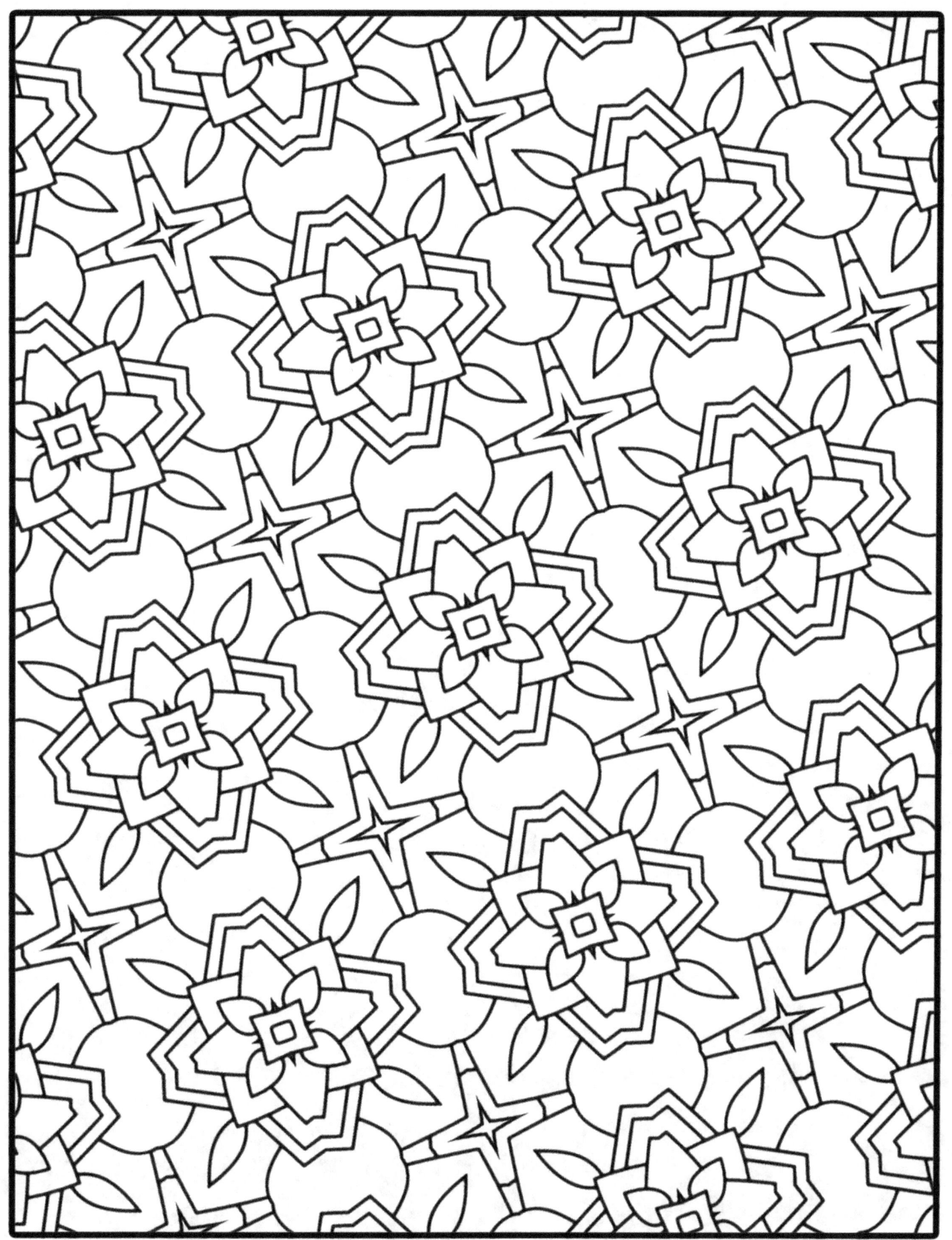

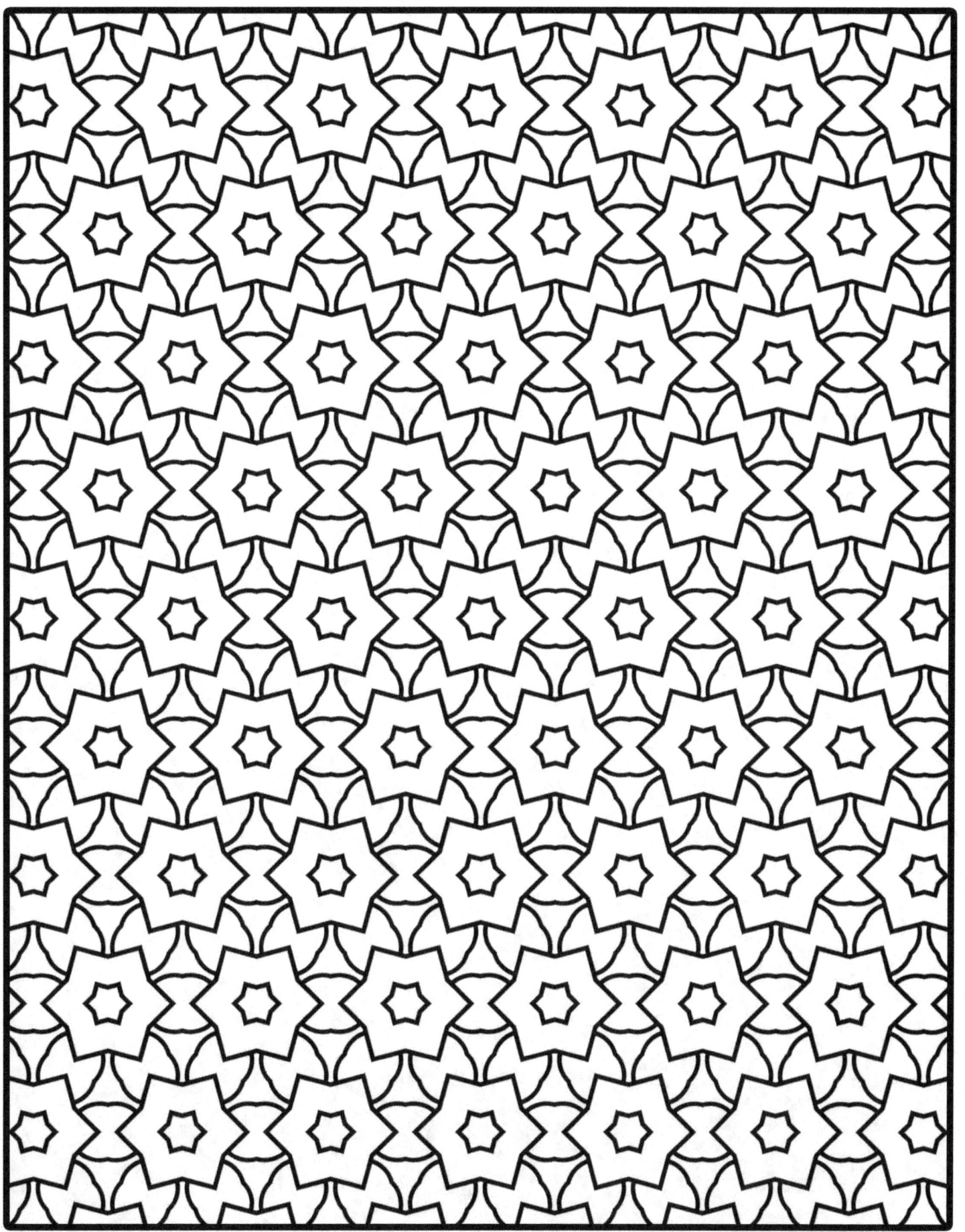

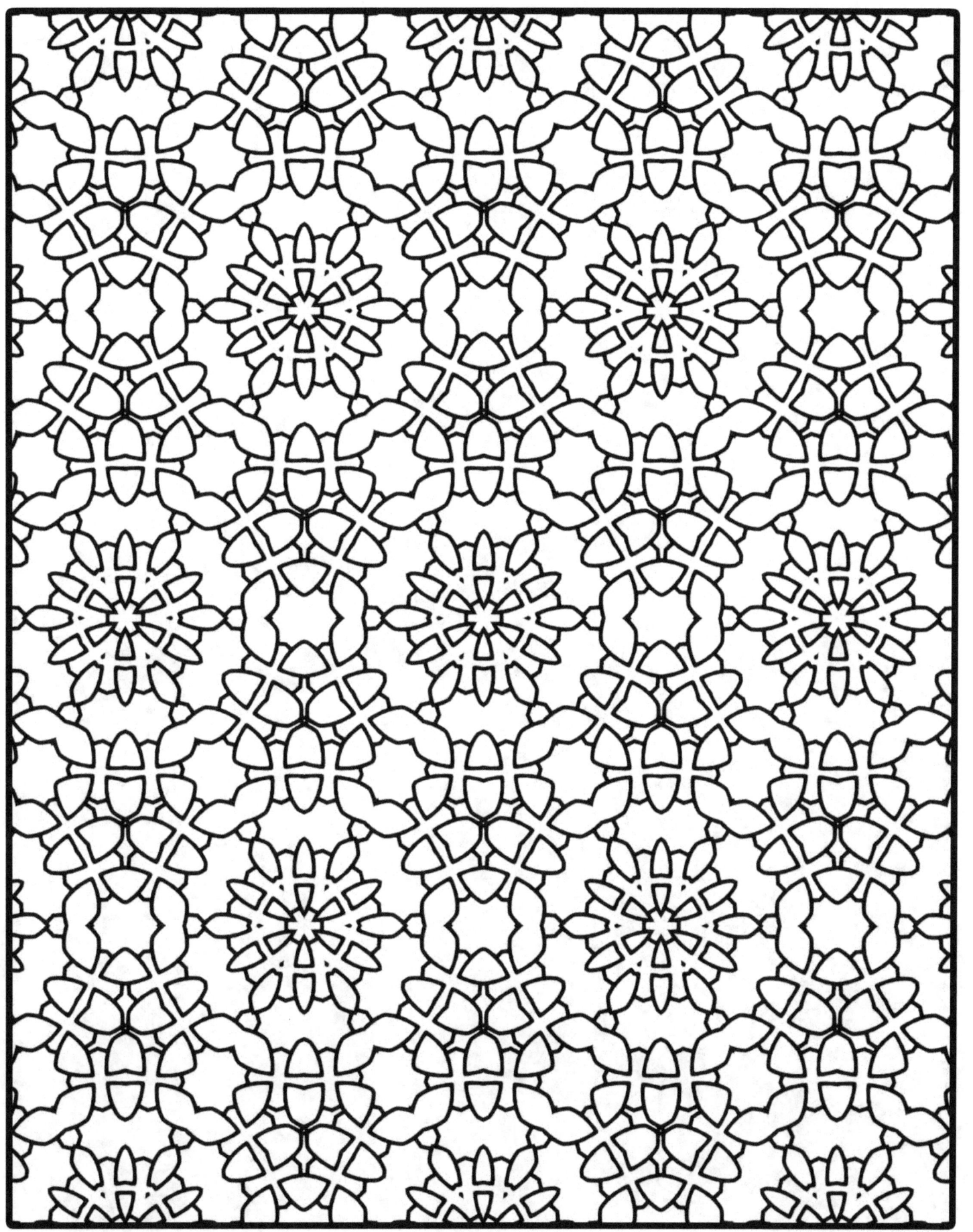

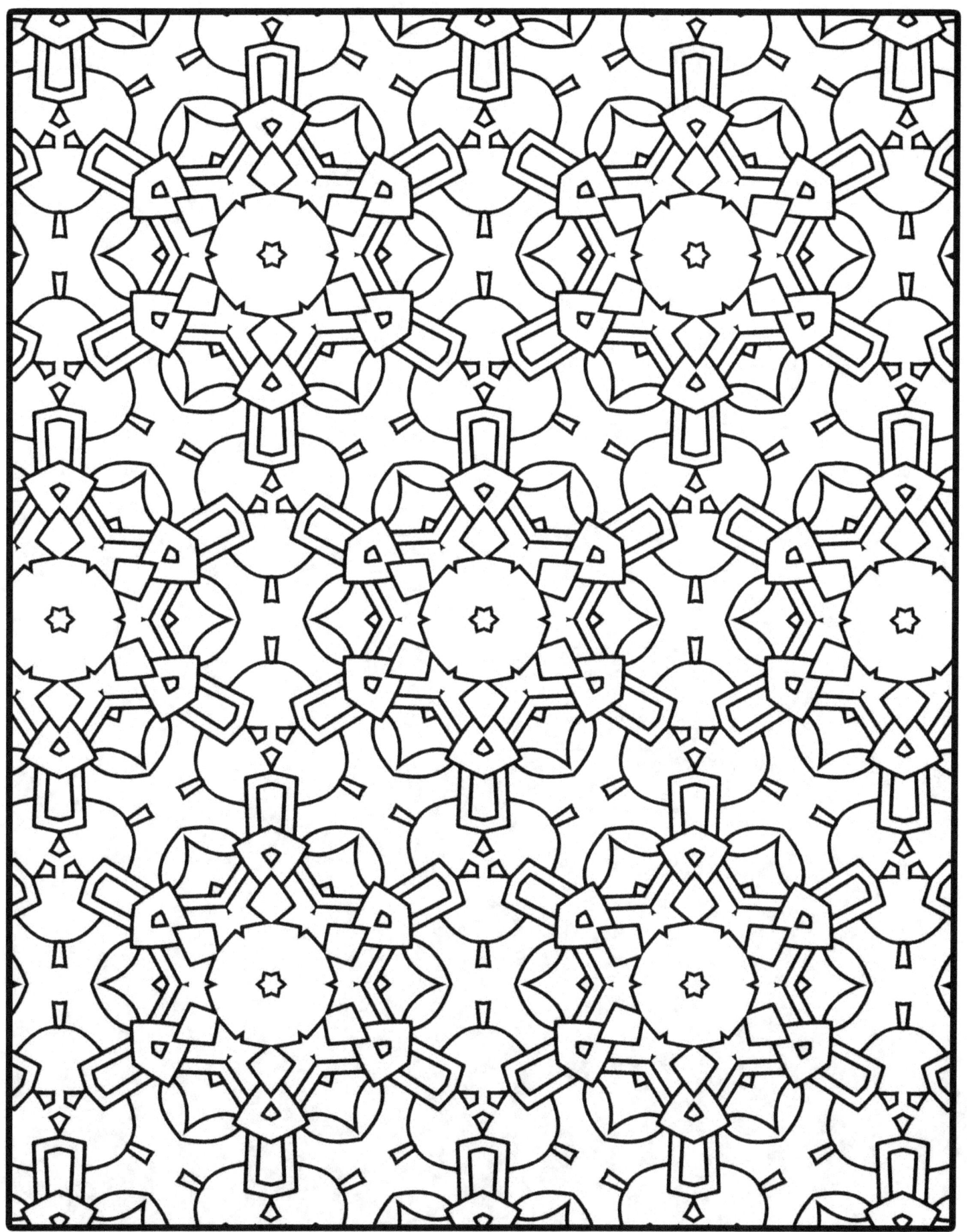

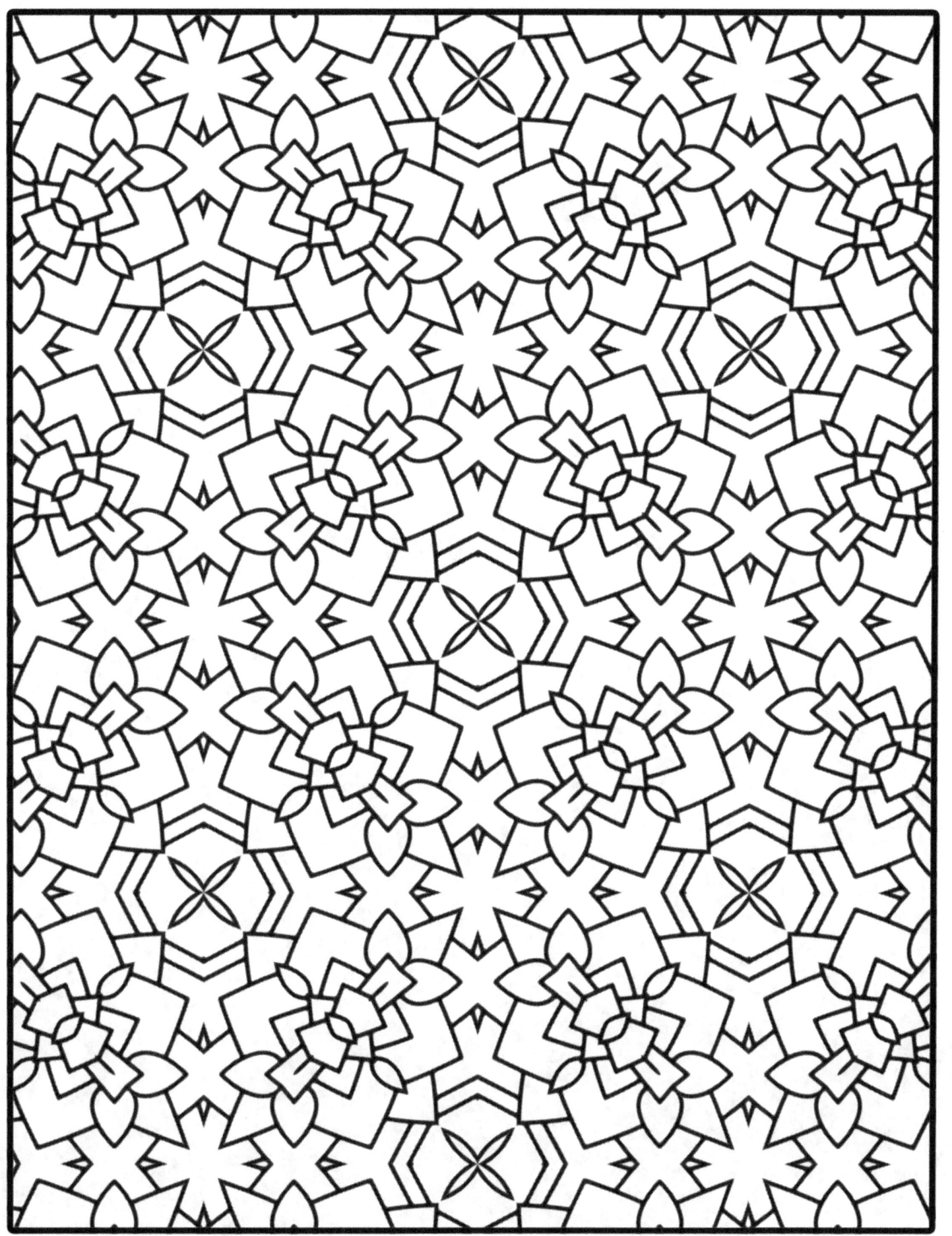

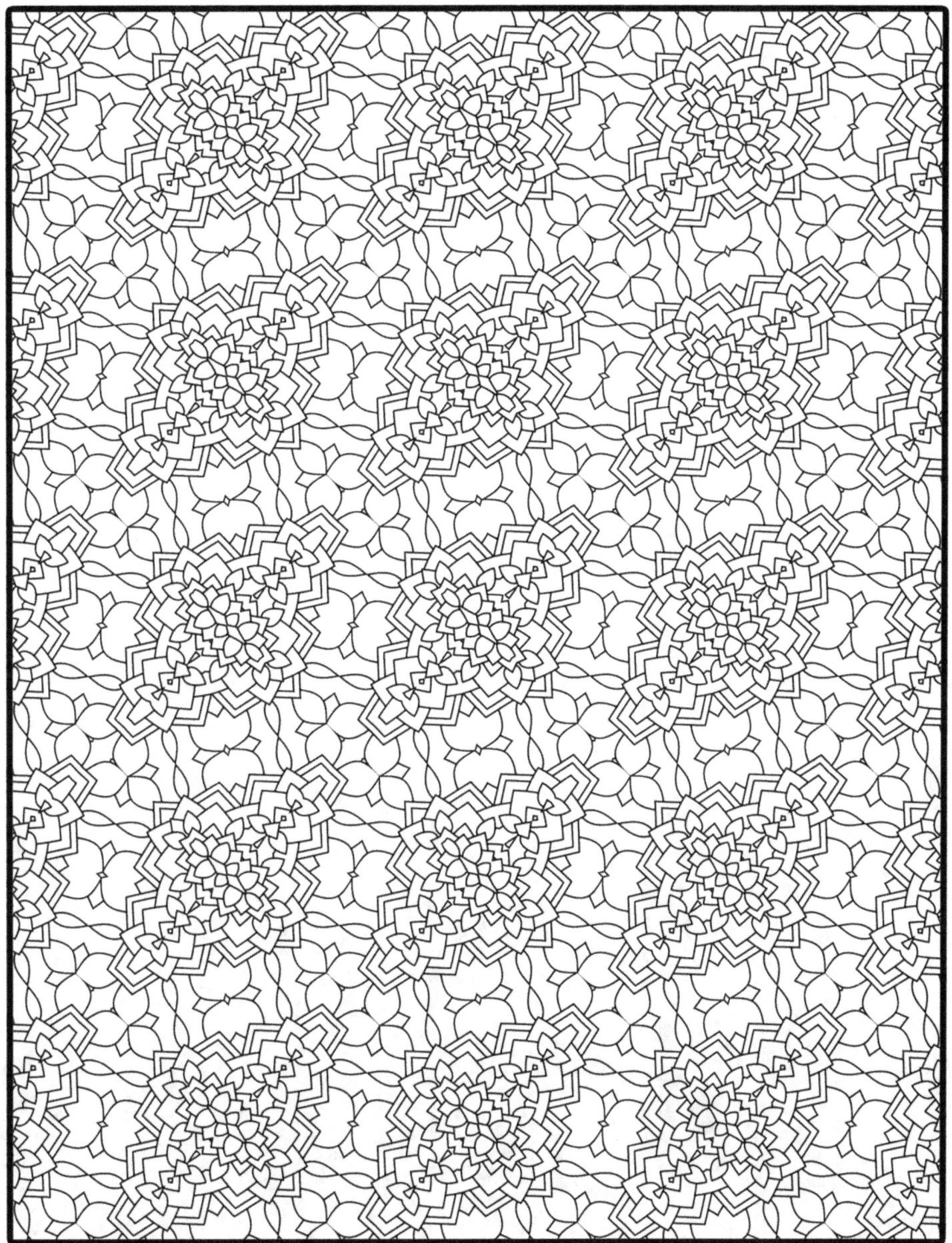

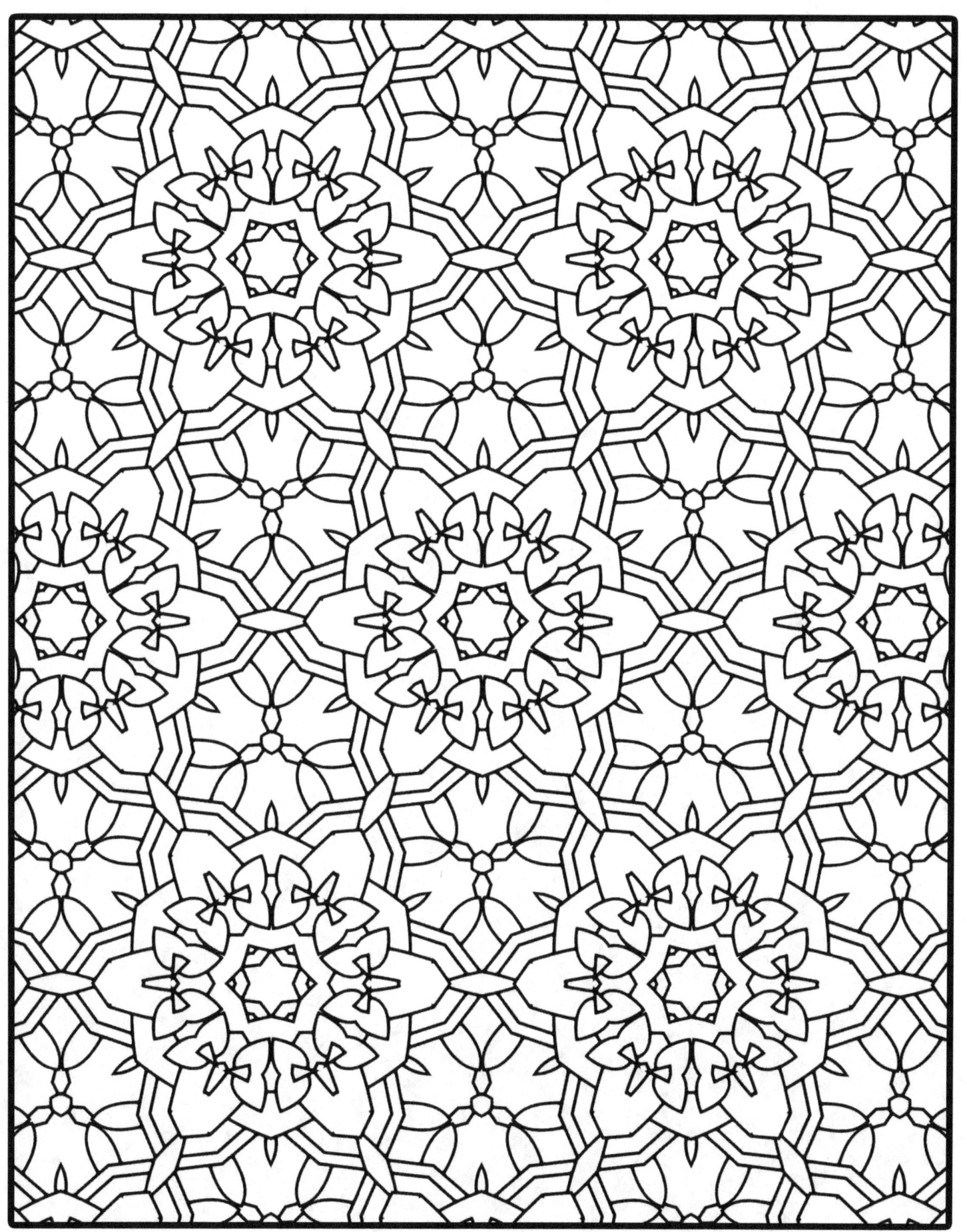

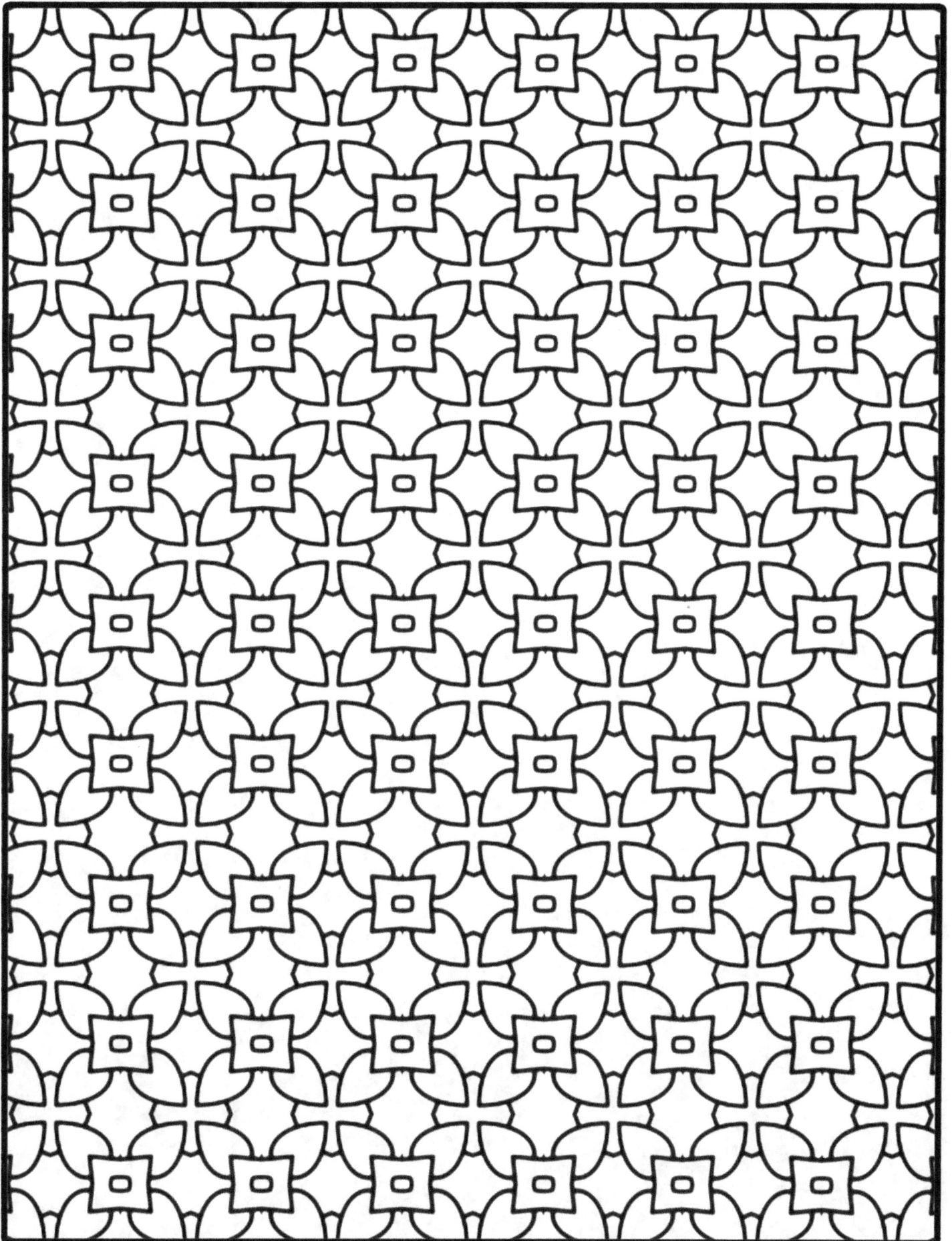

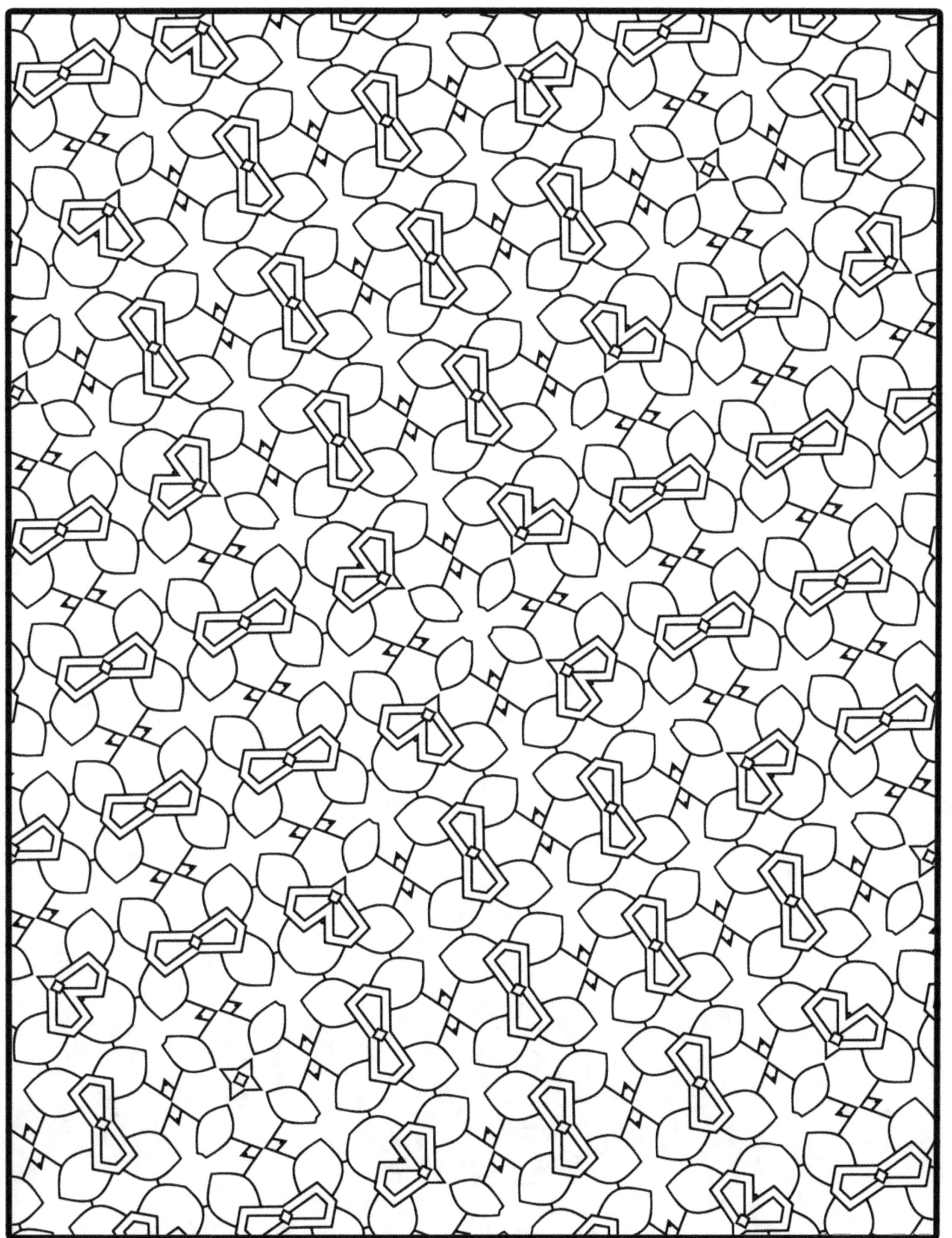

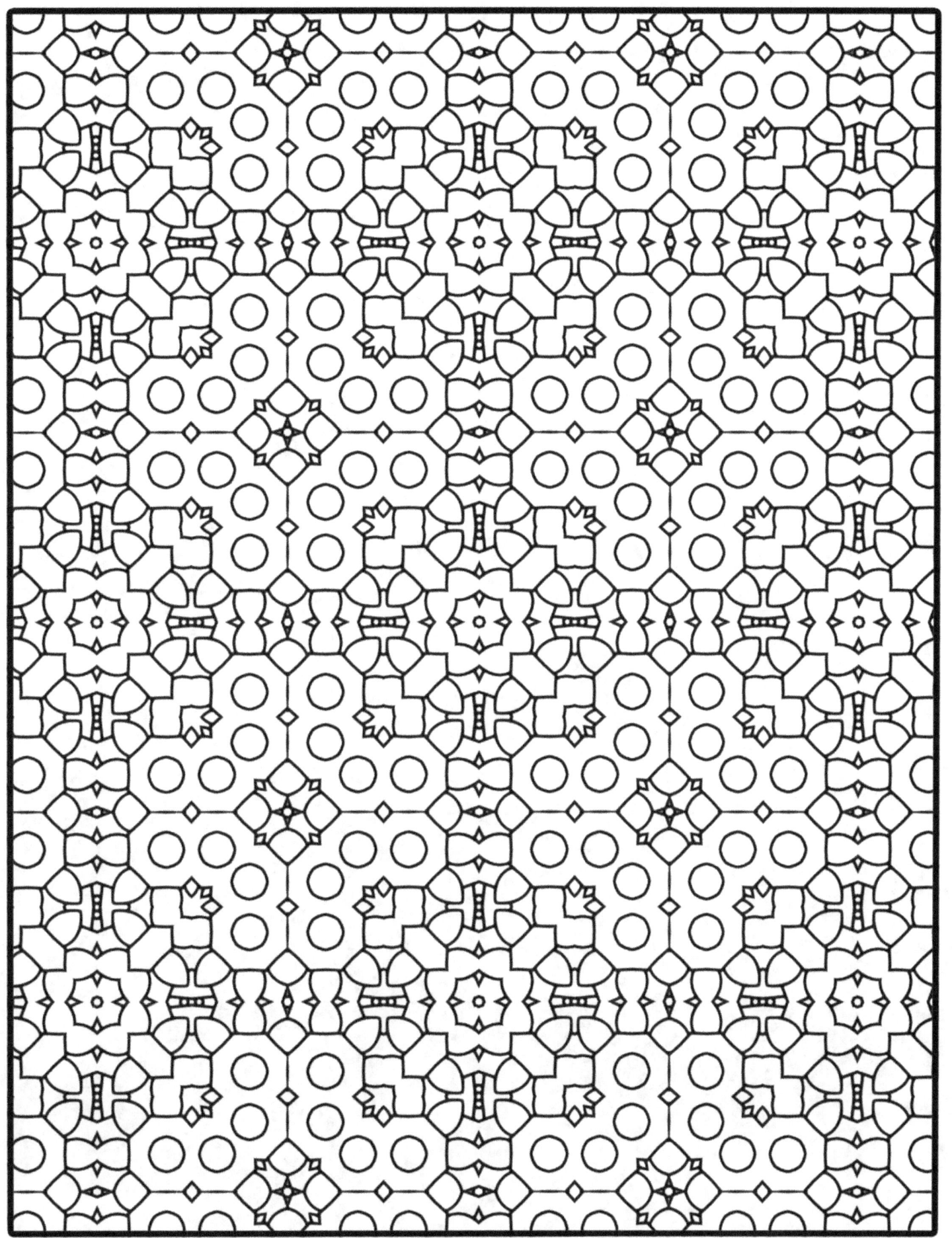

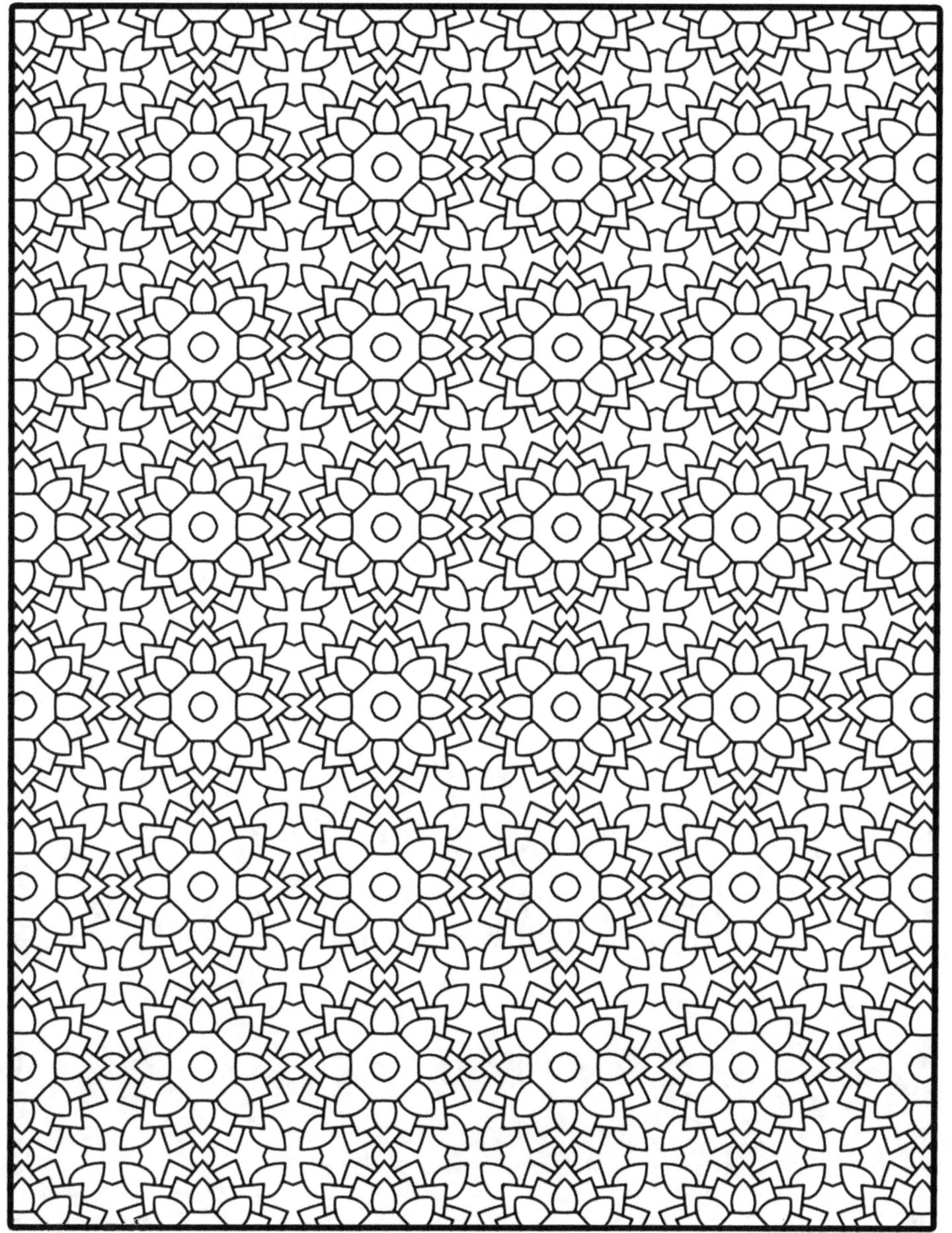

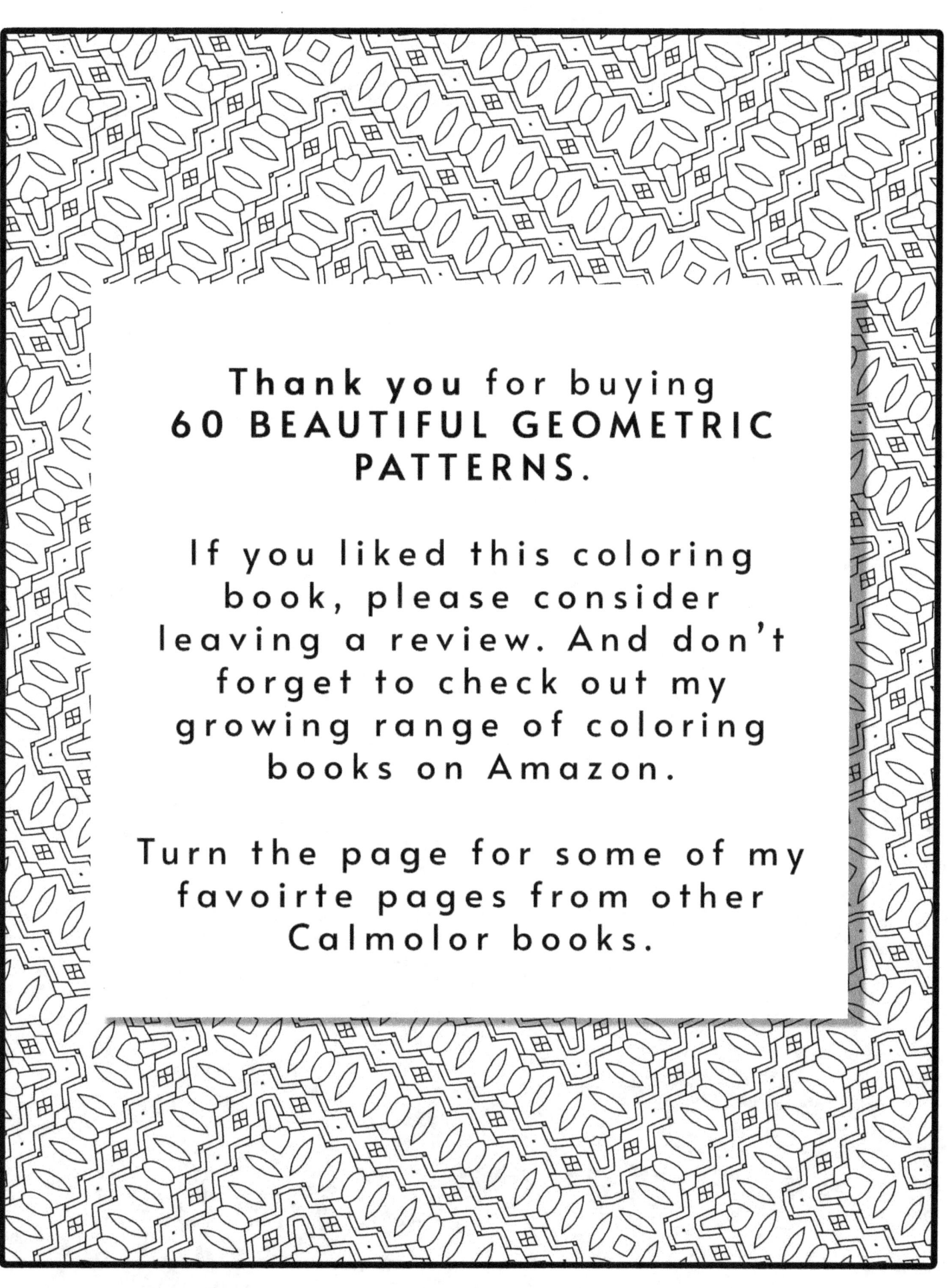

Thank you for buying
60 BEAUTIFUL GEOMETRIC
PATTERNS.

If you liked this coloring book, please consider leaving a review. And don't forget to check out my growing range of coloring books on Amazon.

Turn the page for some of my favoirte pages from other Calmolor books.

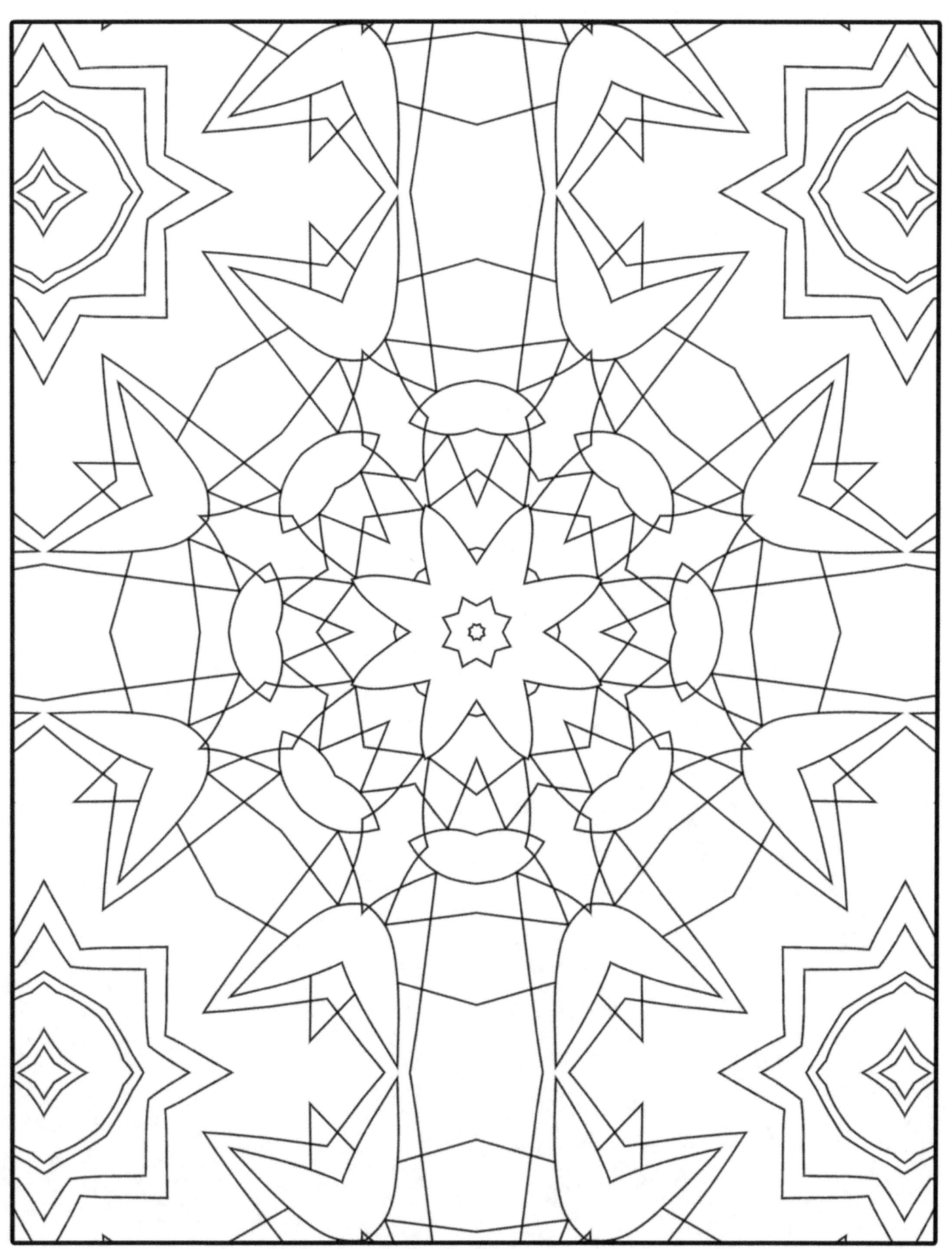

50 BEAUTIFUL BLOOMS

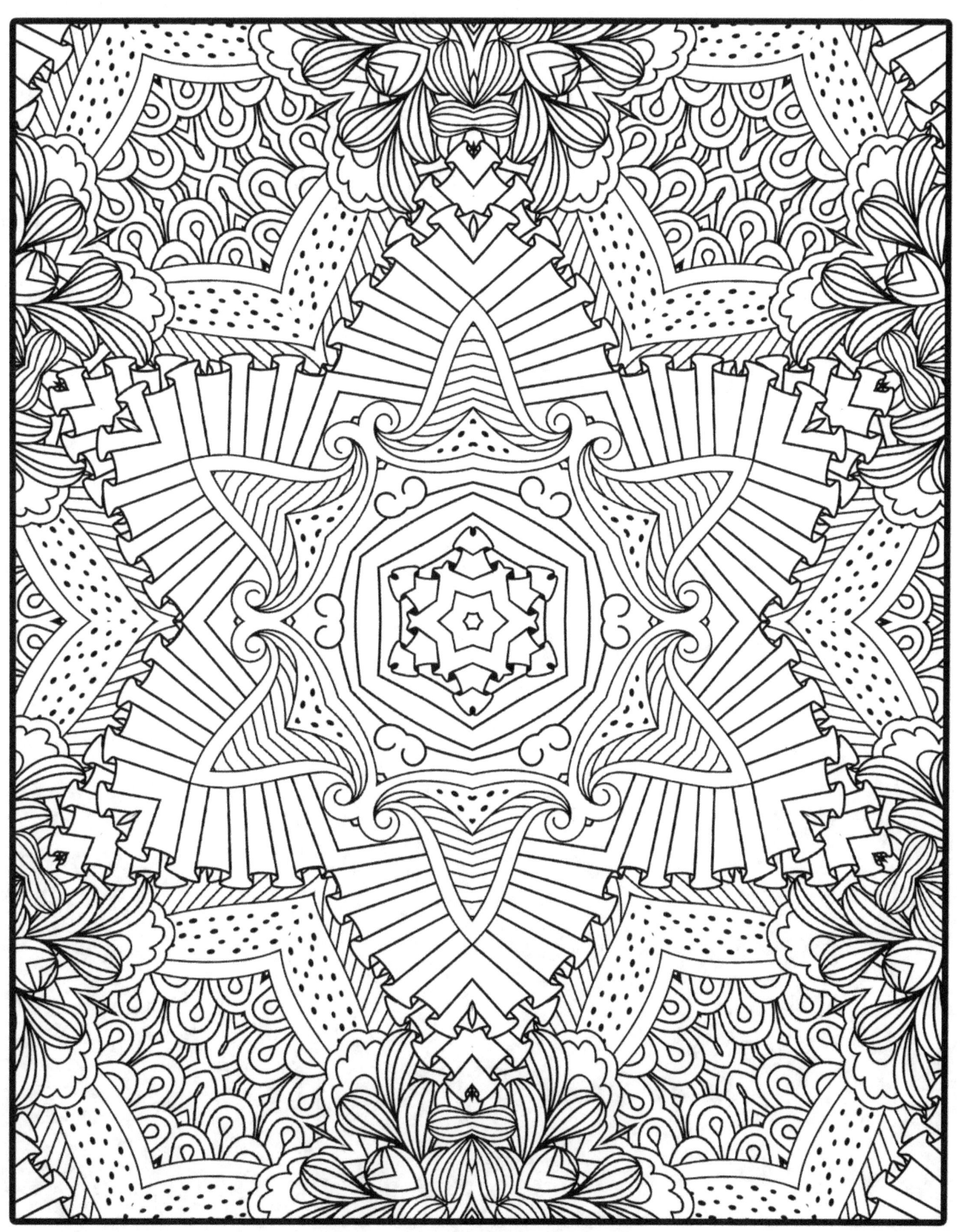

CURLS AND SWIRLS

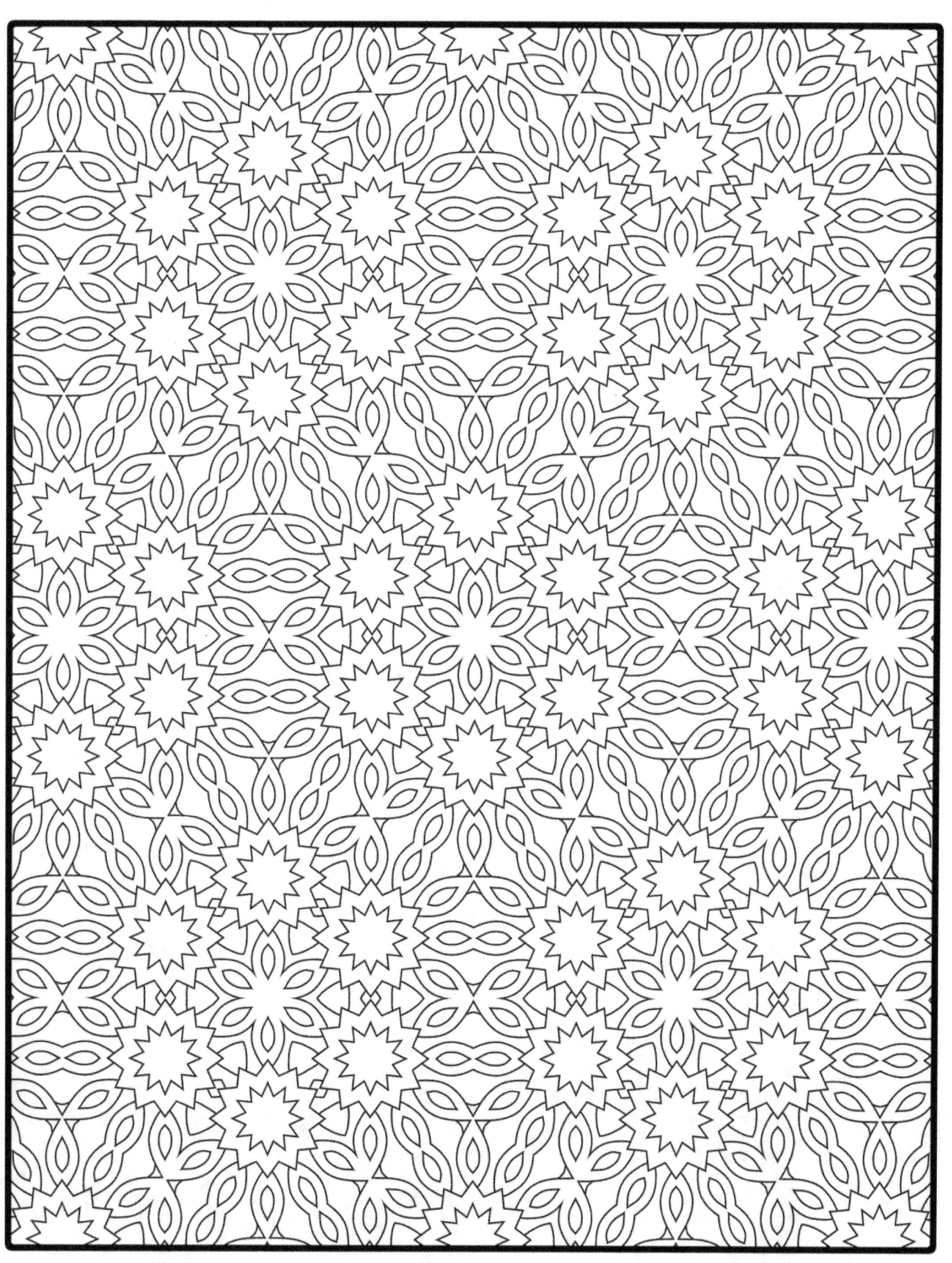

100 EYE-CATCHING PATTERNS

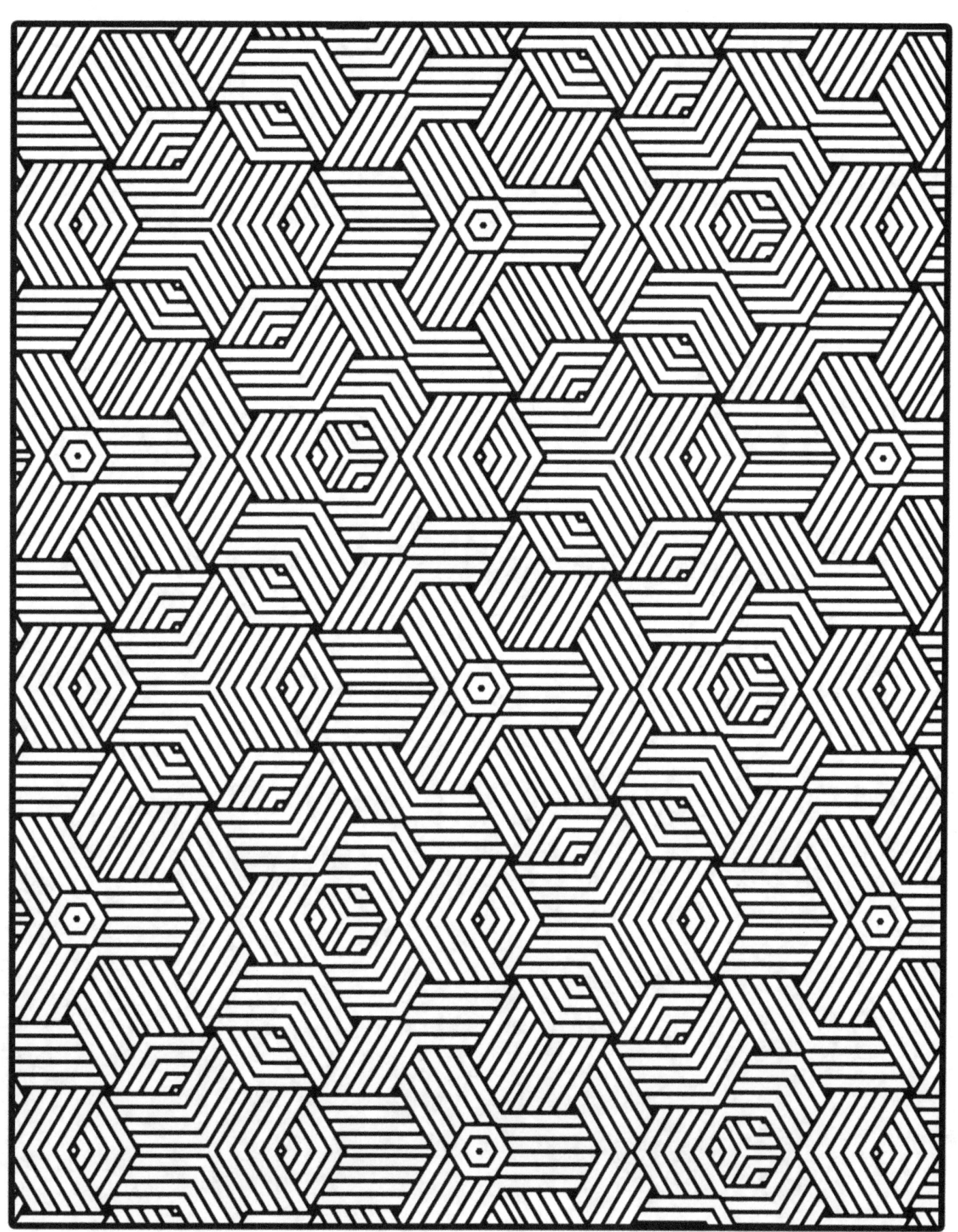

60 BEAUTIFUL GEOMETRIC PATTERNS BOOK 2

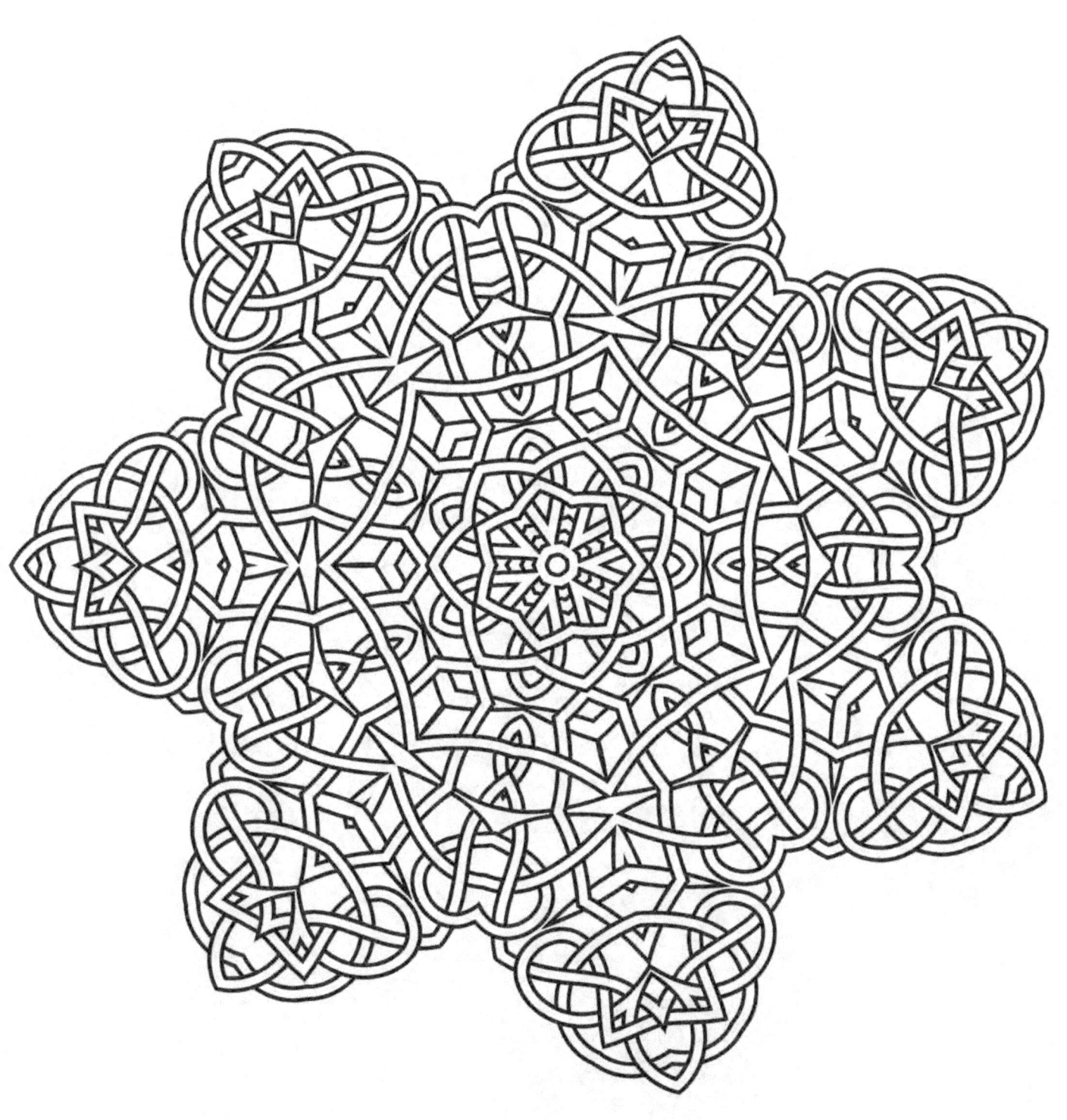

CELTIC KNOT MANDALAS

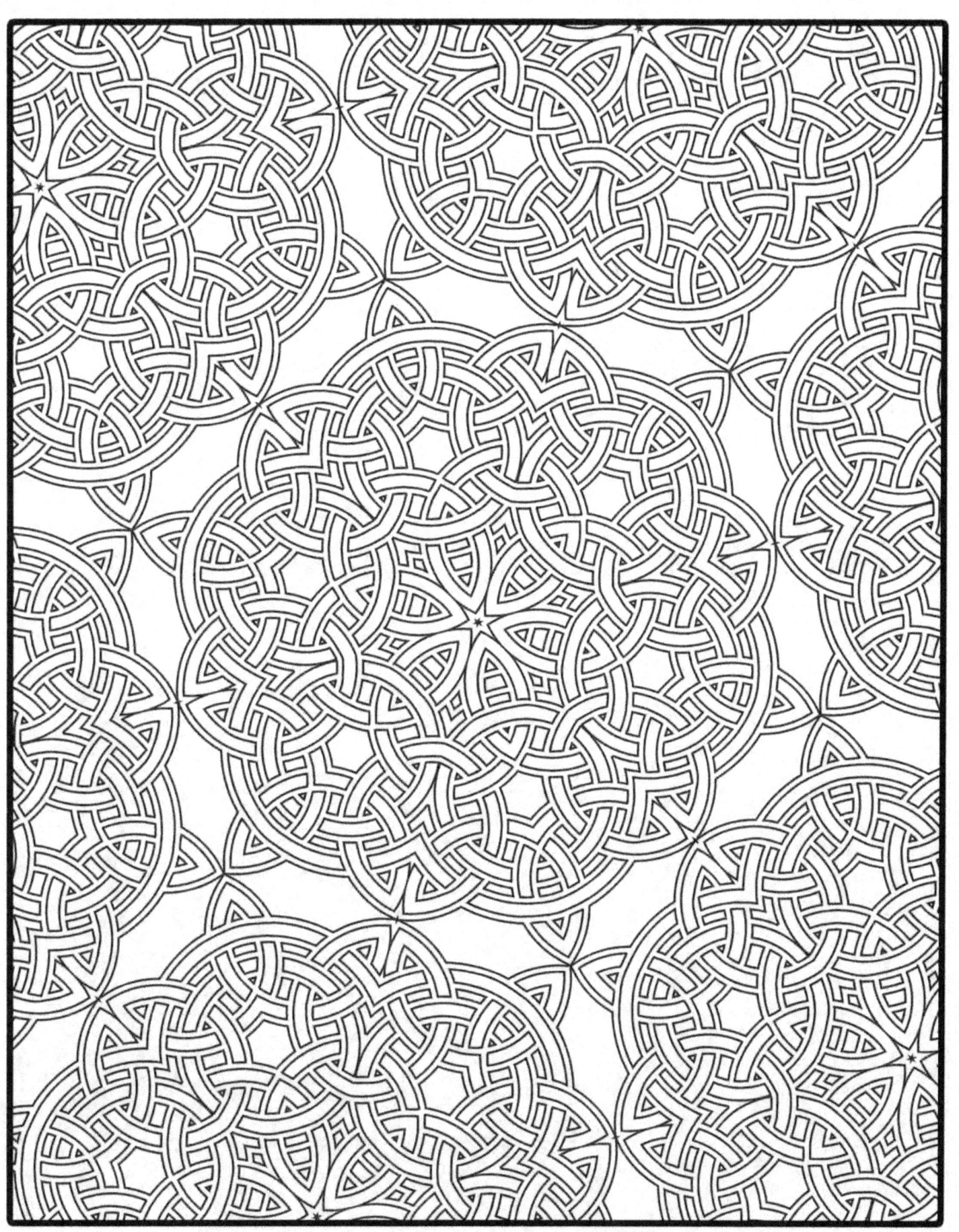

CELTIC KNOT PATTERNS

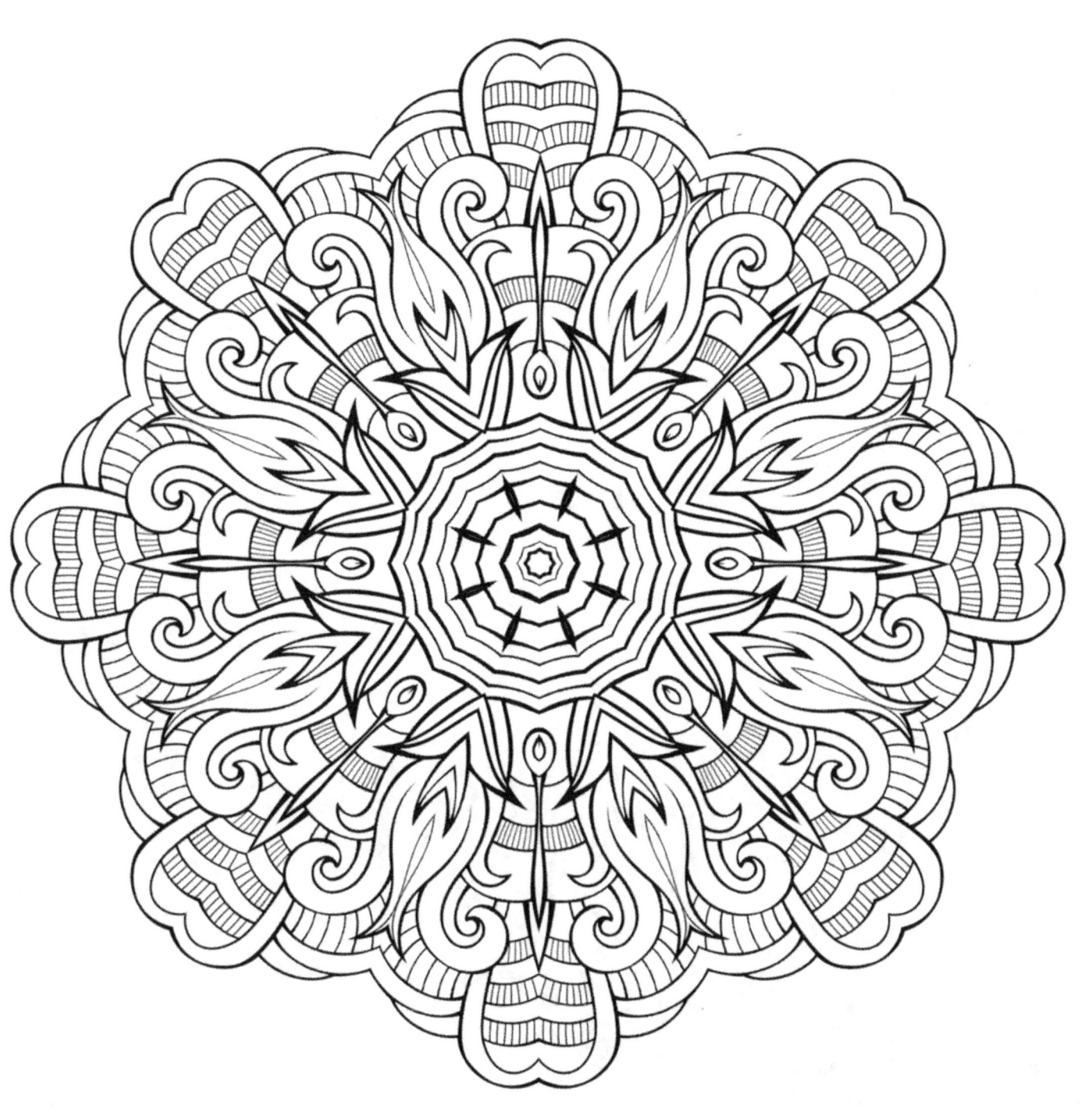

MEDITATIVE MANDALA:
100 BEAUTIFUL AND RELAXING DESIGNS

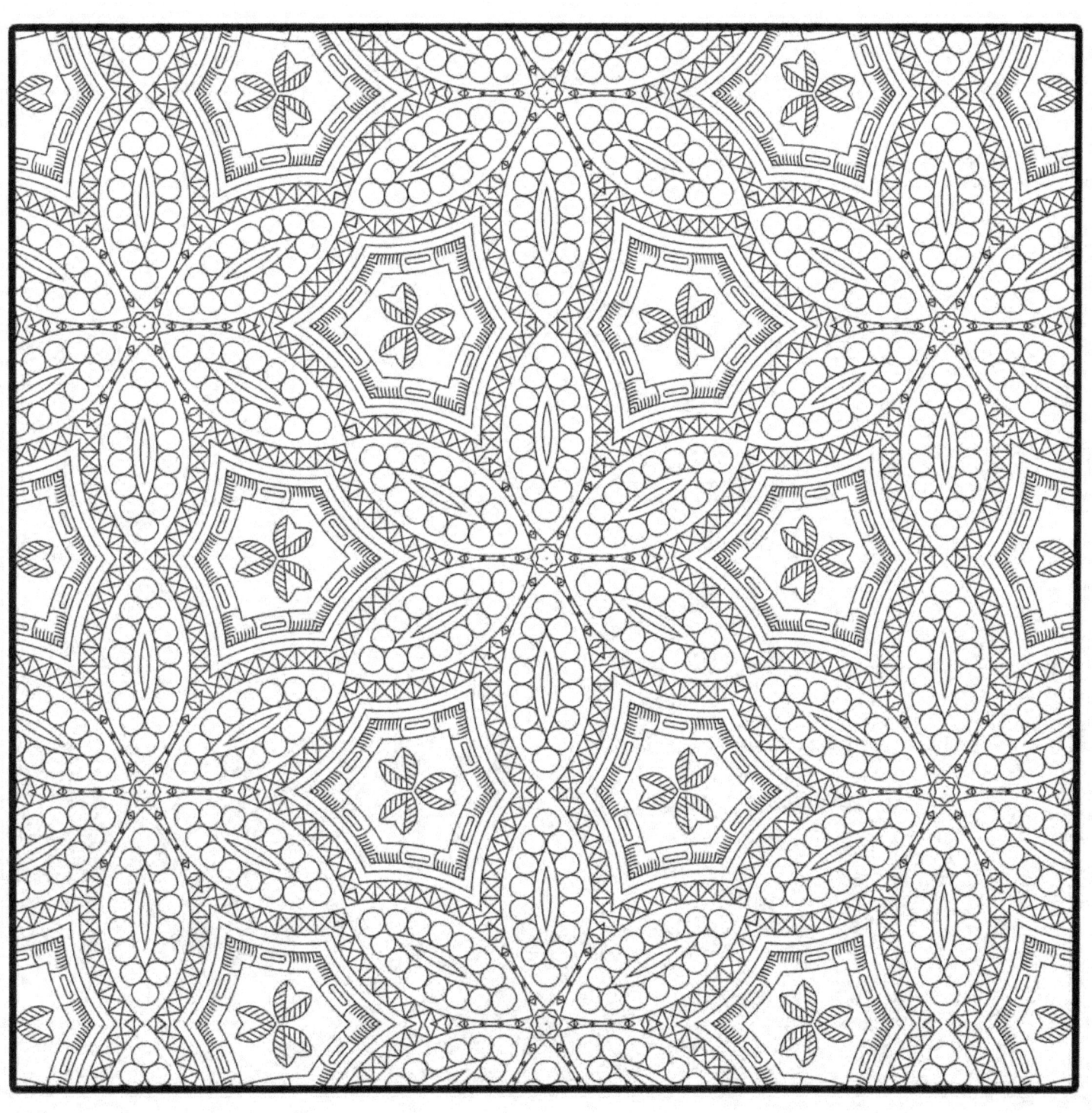

ZEN PATTERNS
50 STRESS-RELIEVING DESIGNS

BACKING PAGE

TEAR OUT

www.ingramcontent.com/pod-product-compliance
Lightning Source LLC
Chambersburg PA
CBHW080833220526
45467CB00008B/2266